HOW TO
BE YOUR
OWN BOSS
as a single mum

BY ALI GOLDS

Single Mum. And her own boss.

Design by John Amy
www.ebookdesigner.co.uk

> "I am only one
> but still I am one.
> I cannot do everything,
> but still I can do something;
> and because I cannot do everything
> I will not refuse to do the something that I can do"

WILLIAM EVERETT HALE

Thankyou again Tracey, wishing you the very best in your business, and personal life :)

love, Trixx

Contents

Chapter 1: Hello!

I never planned to be a single mum. I'm not convinced that many women do. I read articles in certain parts of the media that vilify us as a group; accusing us of fecklessness, of using the benefits system to our own ends, not letting dads see their kids unless we get something out of it, and of raising children who are more likely to be physically weaker, educationally lower achievers, and go on to commit crime in their teens; and I shake my head in astonishment. It's not a world that I recognise.

The single mums I know – and I know a lot – are the hardest working people you will meet. Whether they are in employment, self-employment or staying at home to raise young children, they never have an easy time of it. After all, not only are they trying to keep their own heads above water as well as that of their families – trying to keep everyone happy (kids, other parent, relatives on both sides, the benefit office where appropriate etc) – but they are also trying to live. Not exist. *Live*. And having a life as a single mum, certainly without people thinking they can comment freely on it, can be near impossible.

It's a little easier if you have a support network – friends, family, ex partner still on the scene, perhaps you're even on amicable terms – but if you don't it's incredibly difficult. Of course, there are lots of online networks as well as local groups run by organisations such as Gingerbread, but when I became a single mum back in May 2005, I had no support network. My ex had managed to isolate me from my friends so the only people I knew were his friends; I had distanced myself (for various reasons and with his support) from my mother and siblings, and my father lived abroad. The only people in my life were my kids.

My ex and I had met in late 1995 and married in 1997. Within weeks of our first meeting we were besotted. We thought we'd finally found our soul mates in each other.

We both had children from our previous marriages, and then had a son of our own. We were completely convinced that we had the perfect marriage and partnership and, at the time, we were probably right. We respected each other, supported each other and our worlds centred on each other. I lost count of how many people told me they were envious of what we had. That we were the couple they yearned to be.

In so many ways we were absolute opposites. He was brought up in a tough part of Birmingham, left school at fifteen with a couple of qualifications at the height of the teachers' strikes in the mid 80s, and found a job as a carpenter after his mother threw him out one morning and told him not to come back until he'd got some work.

He was a roughty-toughty kind of man; swore like a trooper, and had questionable views on a number of subjects including women and race. He also liked a drink.

I was brought up in a relatively leafy part of the South Coast. I left school with a couple of O Levels in Music and RE before going back to college to boost my qualifications. I fell into a career in sales, and then some years later, sales and marketing. The perfect job for someone who had the 'gift of the gab' as my parents said. I was perfectly spoken, in fact modelled my accent back then on the cut glass tones of Radio 4 presenters. I was extremely tolerant of everyone – if you hadn't hurt me, I didn't see why I would object to you – and was developing a strong advocacy of women's rights. And as for drinking? Well, I only needed to sniff a cork and I'd fall over, so I never really touched alcohol. Still don't.

Against all the odds, my ex and I hit it off immediately. He was younger than I was, and although looks wise he wasn't the type I usually went for, he was astonishingly charismatic – and I fell for him hook, line and sinker.

He, in turn, whilst telling me he loved me every day, was wowed by my advertising sales job in London, my clients (a smattering of celebrity business owners) and how much I earned; which he liked to brag about to everyone he knew. Oh, and just in case he sounds extraordinarily shallow – he also loved the fact that not only was I tiny in height but also in size: five foot two inches, size 6/8. Apparently he only ever dated small women.

Within a few months we were living together. (I found out afterwards that he had been desperate to escape the Midlands, having been exposed for an affair with the wife of a local hard man.)

We bought a beautiful, very old cottage in a sought after part of Sussex; used his carpentry skills and my love of interior design and sold it for a profit. And then we bought another house – on the river, with a huge garden and loads of indoor space for our combined families.

Life was exquisite.

Having both been working for other people – him for a local joiner, me in London for a dot com – and seeing just what we had achieved for them (and could, therefore, achieve for ourselves), we decided to set up our own bespoke cabinetmaking business in 1999, and opened the doors a few months later in the new millennium.

We started with a small amount of cash and a vast amount of optimism and enthusiasm and after a rocky start, started to make money. We made a profit in our first year and, before we knew it, started bagging some high profile clients, including a premier league footballer and commercial bank.

Life was good.

Although it was principally the two of us working in the business, we took on sub-contractors to help with large jobs when we needed to, and it continued to grow steadily.

We toyed tentatively with another idea, a combination of wooden and leather furniture, but it turned out to be ahead of its time and, as a result, didn't take off.

Still, we knew our main market inside out and decided to concentrate our efforts into developing the company to a point where not only could we move into a larger workshop and take on a permanent team, but also start taking time out for other projects we'd been talking about.

We loved working together, we were a brilliant team and would happily have spent every hour we could developing the company. But, we had a family too, of course, and were both acutely aware that we, and particularly he, were not spending as much time at home as we should due to the pressures of running the business.

Although it really was becoming a family business – my daughter earned pocket money sweeping up at weekends, and all the children came up to the workshop now and again to see what we were doing, as well as attending client parties with us that we were invariably invited to – we needed to start differentiating between work and home.

However, our hard graft was paying off and we were starting to see the fruits of our labour. We both drove fast executive cars, had a beautiful home that was kitted out with our beautiful, trademark, bespoke furniture, and were starting to take much deserved holidays here and there.

But I was getting bored. I wanted a fresh challenge. I love the buzz of the start-up; running an established business doesn't fill me with the same excitement. It's not what I'm good at – in my sales career I was always the hunter, not the farmer. The business developer not the account manager. Besides, I didn't make the furniture and that was obviously a key requirement for whoever worked there. We needed to start being savvy with our money if we were going to take what we were doing to a whole new level. Paying for two directors when one did the lion's share of the work wasn't the solution.

Some six months earlier we had sold our home, the four walls that gave me more security than I had ever felt in any property I'd lived in, and moved into a small rented cottage. We had invested the money we'd made from the sale into the business to grow it, the idea being that we would buy another house in a year or so's time, whilst having taken our company up to the next level we were so keen to reach.

I was fairly sure I could leave my treasured business in the capable hands of my husband and, just keeping an eye on things here and there to make sure that they were ticking over nicely, start up a new venture.

I had my sights set on the Italian property market.

I had seen how cheap property was over there, and knew that we either had, or could lay our hands on, a lot of the skills needed to develop these often tumble-down villas and houses. My idea was that we would sympathetically restore them and then rent them out as total holiday solutions. Top quality furniture and furnishings; even books, CDs, DVDs and bikes for our holidaymakers to use.

I brushed up my rusty Italian and started making enquiries. I wanted to take a solid business case to my husband, sure that he would be as keen as I was. We'd visited Italy that summer and had both loved it.

Much to my surprise, he was staunchly against the idea – and refused to speak to me for days after I'd showed him the plans. He saw my interest in another business as a betrayal of the one we'd built up ourselves. As a betrayal of him. He went from sending me text messages littered with kisses and adoring sentiment, leaving notes around the house for me to find declaring his undying love, to icy cold indifference almost overnight.

He actively discouraged me from visiting the workshop and shooed me out when I did, refusing to update me on job progress and new business opportunities, even though I was a director and shareholder as well as company secretary – with every right to know, and question.

He brought in his best friend to work alongside him, and little by little he came home later and later until he hardly came home at all.

At the same time, he started showing an interest in a very close female member of my family who was living with us. He started spending all of his time with her; collecting her from work and taking her out; turning off his phone when he was with her, and rounding on me in violent anger when I questioned what he was doing… It was my sick mind. My nasty imagination. His actions were innocent and purely platonic.

It was when I found him in bed with her, innocently asleep he said, and he still continued to vehemently deny that anything was going on, that I realised my marriage was over; when he screamed, centimetres from my face, that when she walked into a room it lit up – and when I walked into a room it fell dark. That he had told her that no one loved her except for him.

I gave him seven days to leave our house – and he instantly cancelled my business debit card, refusing to contribute a penny to the household running costs or to discuss maintenance payments once he had left. He also threatened to leave me without a penny to my name, and I had no doubt that he meant it.

Carrying on working in the business, even though we were apart, was a non-starter. We had gone from finishing each other's sentences to him ignoring or baiting me in a matter of weeks. I couldn't step foot in the workshop for fear of what he would say or do, and he'd made it crystal clear that he had no interest in my being there. If he could have banned me from my own business premises, he would have done.

I hated being in my home too, knowing that at any moment the pair of them could walk in and the atmosphere change. That the menace of what was happening right under my nose, even though apparently it wasn't, would just carry on regardless – destroying me, and shattering the lives of my children.

The day he left I lost everything. My job and therefore my income; my car (he decided he wasn't paying for it and I couldn't afford to); my ability to purchase another home (all the money from the sale was in the business and I couldn't afford a lawyer to get what I was owed); my marriage and my much-loved relative. He then refused to pay maintenance for our son, and eventually, after two years, stopped seeing him altogether.

Going, in a matter of weeks, from a relatively comfortable lifestyle with the promise of much better to come, to one where I literally didn't have two pennies to rub together, was a shock to the system; but going from feeling loved and supported to abandoned overnight was the cruellest feeling of all.

It's impossible to explain how utterly devastated I felt. I've tried but there are no words that do it justice. Perhaps there are just no words for it. I had given everything I had to this man; trusted him when I had never trusted anyone else before, loved him beyond love, and made him the centre of my world. He had filled me with happiness and had now left me overflowing with grief.

However, I had a son at home and another living away to support, and I knew that I had no time to dwell on my feelings – I needed to find an income to ensure a roof over our heads so that I wouldn't have to resort to benefits. The idea of walking into the local job centre and completing the long and complicated forms filled me with equal forms of dread and embarrassment. Call it misplaced pride, or just bloody-mindedness; either way, I knew that wasn't a route I could take.

First, I loved working. I couldn't imagine doing anything else. Signing on with the benefits office instead of with a recruitment agency just wasn't on my radar. Apart from anything else, as I've said, the idea of trying to complete the forms alone put me off. I'm dyspraxic, and forms and I just don't go hand in hand. I had no one willing to do them with me or for me. And sitting at home twiddling my thumbs would have given me far too much time to dwell on what had just happened in my marriage – I knew that was a road to disaster. I was in a very fragile mental state. It was obvious to me that I would run the risk of a breakdown if I spent too much time on my own thinking, and then over-thinking. I knew I would literally collapse, which I couldn't allow myself to do. So that was that.

Secondly, I'd seen the lifestyle I could have if I carried on working. At that stage, I had no idea how long it would take me to get back there (and nine years on, I'm still not quite there) but it wasn't going to stop me.

Obviously, working in the bespoke furniture market, we'd created pieces for people with lots of money and for people who'd saved hard to make their homes as gorgeous as they could. I'd seen what money could achieve, and I wanted that for my family.

I'd had the beautiful house in the equally beautiful part of the world. I'd had the fast executive cars and the foreign holidays. I knew what it felt like to have money. I knew the freedom it gave, and the options it offered. The security of knowing that if something broke you could afford to fix it; and that if you carried on working hard, you could replace that money the next month.

I knew how reassuring that all felt. And if I needed anything at that point, it was reassurance.

Thirdly, I was damned if I was going to let my ex get the better of me. I had a sneaky feeling that he wanted me to fail; he wanted me to fall on my knees and not be able to get back up. He wanted to feel that he was the one with the power; he was the one who could carry on achieving and I would just have to watch. That I had only achieved what I had achieved with him leading the way. That on my own I offered nothing.

I don't think so.

Now, I'm not motivated by money but I am motivated by being the best I can be. I'm not motivated by material things but I am motivated by building financial and housing security for myself and my family. I knew that if it wasn't for me, the business we had built would have struggled and, in fact, it did. My ex closed it a year later, transferred the assets to another company, and that closed some two years on. So I knew that, despite my desperate emotional situation – falling asleep in tears, still crying when I woke up for what felt like forever but was in reality the first twelve months, suffering crippling nightmares and memories of my husband and family member together in bed – I had every intention of carrying on. I wasn't going to stop, I wasn't going to give up – and I certainly wasn't going to let a man dictate the rest of my life for me.

And fourthly, I wanted my kids to have a strong role model. To have someone they could look up to and learn from. I didn't want them to see me in pieces, and seemingly unable to cope. They knew how sad I was, they saw the tears – no matter how much I tried to hide them – but I needed them to realise that whatever happens in life, you have to pick yourself up and keep going. Dust yourself down and start walking again.

I wanted my kids to see that, by working, they could achieve anything they wanted because they'd been brought up by a mum who had not only dealt with the emotional and practical results of a relationship breakdown, but had then pulled out all the stops to work too. I wanted them to learn that nothing comes easy and that anything you want takes a serious amount of working at – and it doesn't come the first time around.

That teaches so much.

It shows them life is there to be grabbed with both hands, irrespective of what challenges might lie ahead, and to be lived. That life goes on, and so must you. So I closed down my feelings, went onto automatic pilot, and started looking for work.

I quickly found that if you've worked for yourself, many companies shy away from you. If it's a large company, the manager knows that you probably have considerably more experience than they do, and in a small company the owner knows that you have already done exactly the same as they are doing. Either way, it makes you a threat.

Luckily, I found a local recruitment agency where the manager not only valued my experience but saw it as a package of many years in total, rather than just five years of self-employment. After meeting her to discuss some vacancies that she was currently handling, she offered me a job as a Recruitment Consultant, ending up becoming one of my great friends and, certainly at that point, the only one I had.

I thought that working for someone would be the same as working for myself, the only difference being that I was no longer in charge of my day.

Wrong.

I am often asked by curious, careworn and desperate-to-escape-from-the-daily-grind friends, which is more difficult – working for yourself or working for someone else. That's a very easy question to answer.

Working for someone else.

When you are your own boss, you make the decisions. You decide when you will work, how you will work and, if there are problems at home, you generally have the flexibility to adjust your schedule. If the kids are poorly, you can work from home whilst they are sleeping. At breakneck speed of course but, nonetheless it can be done. The same if there's a problem with childcare.

Of course, if you are ill that's another story. It's a well-known fact that self-employed people can't be ill. It doesn't matter whether you have broken a leg, have the worst strain of flu known to man or just fancy a duvet day (and, let's face it, who doesn't on occasion!), it just isn't going to happen. If you don't work, you don't earn money and, even worse, you let down your clients. One of the cardinal rules of business is that the Customer is King, so you're not going to do anything to jeopardise that relationship. Being ill when you are a solo entrepreneur – well, you just don't have the time.

It's a whole different story when you work for someone. There's no juggling of childcare and work; no taking days off if your kids are ill. At least not for the company I worked for. And actually, my work ethic is such that the kids would have had to be half dead before I let them take a day off school in any case, but if they really were ill? I had to take the day off too, and frantically re-work my personal financial budgets to figure out where I could afford to lose a day's pay.

In reality I couldn't, so something had to give. Usually food.

I had only been working for a few months when I shut the tip of my finger in the car door outside the childminder's house. I won't bore you with the gory details (the pain was a good 15/10!) but, following an evening in A&E with much wincing from the nursing staff when they saw it, I returned home – driven by my lovely boss who had raced over to my house to take me to the hospital when she heard what I'd done – with a heavily bandaged hand.

Knowing that I wouldn't get paid if I didn't go in to work, and being acutely aware that no money meant no rent payment and no supper, I gingerly drove in the next day and spent the time trying to work but finding it increasingly difficult.

Now, as a couple, it might be easier to deal with this kind of scenario, but as a single mum I had to tough it out and carry on. And the only way you can carry on is to toughen up.

Childcare was another huge problem. I'd never needed to worry about it before. I'd managed to juggle work and my family relatively well. There was a fabulous local nursery school that my son attended most mornings and my older children often helped out when they could, so the perils of finding childminders and holiday schemes hadn't been something that had interrupted my daily thoughts.

Living in a small town on the edge of the South Downs has its plusses, of that there is no doubt, but one of them is not accessible and plentiful childcare. There were only two childminders in the local area. Both of them were full, with waiting lists. The nearest available space was eighteen miles away from my home – and work was twelve miles in the opposite direction. There were no after school clubs, and no holiday schemes unless your child was sporty (mine wasn't) or you only worked from 10am to 12 midday (I didn't).

I found myself dropping my son at school well before the day started, relying on the support and goodwill of the headmaster, and collecting him from the childminder at 6.30pm. This was assuming the traffic was behaving of course, and my car too – otherwise I then had to pay a late penalty and double the hourly rate, which I absolutely couldn't afford.

Of course, my ex had taken my car and refused to help with sourcing another, or even contribute a few hundred pounds towards purchasing a replacement, so I'd had to borrow some money. Just the thought of it gave me nightmares. I hate owing money, so I'd borrowed the smallest amount possible that would allow me to buy something relatively trustworthy. That poor car, an old Renault Clio that had seen many better days, was thrown up and down dual carriageways and tiny country roads every day in my desperate effort to keep a roof over our heads and food on the table.

My evenings were spent recovering from my days, and trying to make sense of what had happened to my life. Wondering how it could have gone from blissfully happy to desperately miserable in a matter of weeks. Trying to keep smiling for my children, yet crying inside.

This manic life eventually started taking its toll on my health; not only was I literally pulling my hair out but I started making stupid mistakes due to the sheer magnitude of what I was experiencing, both work wise and emotionally. I walked into things, dropped things, burnt myself countless times, lost my voice six times in twelve months 'due to the stress' pronounced my doctor, who proffered me antidepressants (which I refused point blank) when I visited for the umpteenth time.

You name it, I did it.

I realised that work was not working. I needed an income but it was increasingly difficult for me to juggle the demands of working for someone else. The demands of 'you must be in the office at this time' and 'you must collect your son at this time' were proving impossible for me to cope with.

School holidays were a nightmare. Not only was there nowhere to send my son – the childminder didn't have the full-time vacancy he would have required, and I wouldn't have been able to afford it if she had – but he was worried about being anywhere that was unfamiliar. He pleaded with me not to send him to a faceless sports centre with children who were strangers. My only option? To ask my ex and his new partner – my relative – to help. So she stepped in, and looked after my son through the six weeks he was off school. Going to their flat, and having to speak to her, hearing all about how my son had loved spending time with her, and how much they missed each other, whilst missing her myself more than I could say, broke my heart and was a reminder of all that I had lost.

My son had also developed a nervous tic as the result of my marriage break-up and the loss of his siblings and father and, whilst he was the sweetest, most stoic little boy you could ever hope to meet, he was just that. A little boy. His need for me, and for some stability in a seemingly mad world, wouldn't allow me to justify the crazy way my life was headed.

During one of my many broken nights, I suddenly realised what I had to do. I had that lightbulb moment. I was going to turn the problems on their head and go back to running my own business. It was the answer to the childcare issues; I could work around my son, and it would give me the time I needed with him to help re-build his confidence and sense of security. I had the skills to set up a company, I already knew that, and I had worked in business development for my entire career (some twenty years at that point) so I was a pretty good salesperson. I could make an idea fly. And I had just the idea.

Whilst working in recruitment for the last nine months, I'd investigated a new form of revenue for the company but they had decided that, as it wasn't part of their core business, they weren't going to take it forwards. This seemed mad to me as I'd proved a business case and made them some money from it, with the potential for much more to come. And I'd made some great contacts too.

Still – if they weren't going to do it...

I resigned just before Christmas 2005, much to everyone's bemusement (what about the job security and regular income? You're a single mum!), but I left the office on my last day with the biggest of smiles and a head full of plans. A sense of purpose, and a renewed vigour. The last few months had left me feeling so low, almost depressed, and this had given me the kick I needed. It was the path forwards and the challenge that would help to lift me out of the desperate sadness that engulfed me most days. Even when I wasn't thinking about it, it was there hanging over me. I knew that potentially this could be the biggest mistake I'd ever made – giving up a permanent income for one that would be hit and miss at the best of times, with the only person bringing any money into my house being me. But I was sure that I could make it work. And as it was down to me, I was just going to work and work, and work some more, until the money came in. I wasn't going to be beaten. Not by anyone. Not for anything.

Over the week between Christmas and New Year, I cleared out my daughter's old room, and my sons and I turned it into an office. Not long afterwards, I found my youngest sitting at the kitchen table drawing me an 'open' and 'closed' sign for the door. Knowing that this little boy who had been through so much had the belief in me that I could do it, that I could make this germ of an idea happen, spurred me on even more. He had been let down enough – there was no way that I was going to add to that.

The doors opened for business straight after New Year, and within a week I had brought on a dozen vacancies and as many jobseekers. Despite the initial activity showing that the idea was promising, it was a tough slog making the figures add up. Although I made my first placement, and therefore raised my first invoice by the end of week two, it was far from plain sailing. I only just about made ends meet for the first couple of months by running my own agency and working freelance for another to bolster and secure my income. I was flying by the seat of my pants a lot of the time, but I had faith in what I was doing and in what I knew I could do, and instinctively I just kept going. It might have been tough financially but it wasn't any harder than I was used to. Having started two other businesses previously, I knew what to expect and, crucially, what to do about it. Dig deep and keep going.

However, the plusses were innumerable. I wasn't constantly chasing my tail, rushing from school to work to childminder to home; I was able, in the main, to plan my work around my son and to spend the time with him that he needed. I'm not going to pretend that I was supermum and say that I had lots of creative tasks and exciting projects lined up for him to have a go at when he got home from school so that I could fit another hour or so of work in. I didn't. How fantastic it would be if I had had the time to do that – and the capabilities! I didn't, and I don't. I have to admit to having used the TV and other electronic devices here and there whilst I made phone calls. He came and sat with me whilst I was emailing and we chatted, or he did some homework. I kept the office door open so that I could keep an eye on him, and the office looked out onto the garden so I could see him when he was outside.

Did I feel guilty? Yes. Should I have done? Honestly? No. I had to bring money in, and no one else was helping so I did what I had to do – irrespective of what other people might have thought (and I could hear the disapproving voices in my head all the time) and what they actually said to my face. Quite frankly, I couldn't give a damn. If they weren't going to help then I was just going to do it the only way I knew how.

Sometimes, we put an awful lot of pressure on ourselves to be the perfect parent – and in the real world that just isn't possible. Particularly not if you have to work. I realised that the quicker I accepted this, and stopped feeling so horribly guilty, the better.

And this is how my sons and I lived for the next year. Muddling along, making the best of the hand I'd been dealt. It gave me the breathing space I needed to deal not only with my emotions at my marriage breakdown but with the emotions of them both, particularly my youngest. Financially it wasn't the Holy Grail; I certainly didn't make lots of money but I made more than I had when working for someone else, and that gave me one less thing to worry about.

But do you know what the best outcome was? Forget the money, forget the flexibility, forget the slightly slower pace of life. Running my own business gave me back my confidence. Or at least a significant part of it.

I was crushed when my husband left. Emotionally destroyed. I couldn't understand what had happened; one minute everything was OK, the next everything was over. My brain couldn't comprehend it, much less my heart, and I felt totally and utterly useless, worthless and hopeless. I couldn't see a way forward through anything – but with my renewed confidence? Well, that made a real difference.

I felt I could raise my gaze from the ground and look people in the eye again. I could hold my head up when I left the house and they would see a person who was worth talking to, not someone who was destroyed and of no interest. (Of course they never saw that, but in my state of complete devastation, I was convinced that they did.) I felt that I was more worthy of walking around in the sunshine, of breathing the same air as everyone else. That I wasn't some kind of idiot who had sleep-watched her marriage disintegrate in front of her eyes; let her husband and much-loved family member walk away and not do anything. That I had a right to be out there as much as the next person; that it wasn't my fault. Oh my goodness, the guilt that it was indeed all my fault. It consumed me day and night.

Running my own business and being treated like anyone else in a commercial situation gave me back my sense of self and my self-esteem. No-one knew my personal situation unless I told them. They just saw Ali, business owner. I realised I was powerful. I had a problem; I fixed it. I had an issue; I faced it head on and sorted it out. I had a success; I looked in the mirror and celebrated it. Actually, I celebrated any success by dancing around the sitting room – I still do, much to my son's embarrassment – but I also told myself I was a star. That I deserved to be proud of what I'd achieved, and that now I was going to move on and create more success.

I was my own mentor. I couldn't trust anyone else with my feelings, they were too fragile. In fact, if anyone said anything even vaguely critical it knocked my confidence back to square one. But I got stronger and I got bolder, and I raised the bar a bit more and a bit more until I was out there with the best of them; head to head with established recruitment agencies and winning business. It was one of the most empowering times of my life.

That first foray into solo self-employment made me realise that I could be the person I wanted to be; the nurturer and the provider. That I could juggle work and family responsibilities on my own, and not have to worry about relying on others (who invariably let me down). That I could move my life forwards.

I came to realise and, perhaps strangely to some, embrace the fact that life is unfair. Some of us have more than others. Some of us have advantages that others don't. We are all different and not all equal. The quicker we can accept this, the quicker we can assess what we have and what we don't have; what we need to do to get where we want to get, and prepare to get there. And then get there!

Life is definitely not fair for single mums but that doesn't mean that it can't be incredibly successful, fulfilling and packed with experiences, new people, and achievement. After all, single mums are probably the most entrepreneurial group of people I come across in my new life as an start-up coach and mentor. They just don't know it.

Developing entrepreneurial skills

Towards the end of that first year I found that, although I loved working for myself – as I knew I would – being on my own twenty-four hours a day was really tough. I'm quite a sociable person and I missed the interaction with others. I didn't network (big mistake) and would sometimes go days without talking to anyone apart from my sons. Email didn't count.

I had worked, briefly, for a national enterprise education company and found that not only did I love working with teenagers – they fired my imagination – but I also loved being in an educational environment. Following some encouragement from colleagues and friends, I decided to study for a Post Graduate Certificate in Education so that I could work as a college lecturer. Teaching is a perfect career for a mum. As a lecturer, I would be around much more for my son and not have to panic about holiday scheme arrangements or childminders.

Given my experience in business, it seemed logical that I would teach Business and Management. I had this idea that I would encourage the rows of sixteen and seventeen-year-olds before me to set up their own businesses. I was particularly keen to persuade the girls to think about self-employment, given the flexibility that I knew it could offer to mums with caring responsibilities. Not that, for one second, I saw masses of potential mums in front of me, far from it. I just knew from bitter experience that life can change in the blink of an eye, and the more prepared we are the better. The more strings of skills we have to our work bow, the more able we are to cope with what life throws at us. Better to be economically independent than dependent was my feeling.

I was so naïve! I had absolutely no idea that sixteen-year-olds ran their own businesses! But they did. They do. And they were in my classes. They would queue up to ask my advice at the end of the lesson. They saw the potential for free business advice and support from someone who had been there and done it many times – and I would spend as much time with them as they needed. Before long the word had spread, and students who weren't studying with me were queuing up too.

I was more than happy to help where I could; advice on business plans, what to say to the bank manager, even settling disputes on business ideas between parent and child (which made for a couple of sticky parents' evenings…). I ran sessions every few weeks, but quickly realised that a more permanent and ongoing support solution was needed.

I did some research and found that there was nothing out there, at that time, for teenage entrepreneurs who were in full-time education. This seemed odd. Lots of time and effort was being poured into enthusing young people to be enterprising and entrepreneurial but no one had thought about what to do with these fabulous ideas and potential companies once the 'experts' had left at the end of the day. What about the students who wanted to actually experiment with the ideas they'd developed, and turn them into a business venture? Who was going to help them? I took a few days to consider this dilemma, and the answer came to me.

I was.

I loved teaching with a passion but my career lasted only two years. The lure of running my own business again was too strong, and the opportunity too good to miss. Working with these inspirational teenagers had fired my enthusiasm through the roof and reminded me of all the things I loved about working for myself – and the things I didn't much like about working for other people. I couldn't walk away and leave it to someone else to develop. So, I resigned my lecturing post, cashed in my very small teachers' pension, and set up my office. I was off and on a mission. I am an entrepreneur at heart. This was my baby. Watch me make it fly.

With some encouragement from colleagues and friends, particularly the brilliant team at Oxford Brookes University who were working in the South East developing the entrepreneurial spirit in Further Education, I set up Operation Enterprise in May 2011 to support and mentor student entrepreneurs with their business ventures, as well as staff who were involved in enterprise delivery in colleges. It started small, a delivery day here, a consultancy day there, but before I knew it I was being hired to deliver services on behalf of other organisations working in the same market – all of whom wanted the benefit of my small business experience, as well as my teaching background.

The company quickly grew and I brought in coaches and trainers to work with me, moving into other complementary services including staff training and development. We developed our programmes – 'Start up for Success' for those who wanted to set up a private enterprise, and the 'Social Enterprise Education' (SEEd) programme for those more interested in developing community projects and charities.

Over the months, whilst delivering the programmes in a wide variety of schools and colleges, I started to realise that the majority of students coming along were male. They were full of enthusiasm and passion, with ideas that they were willing to explore to the max, and very definite that they were going to achieve. If it didn't work, it didn't work. They weren't going to worry about it, they were just going to get back up and start again.

The few girls who came along were less confident, certainly about their ideas, and often exhibited self-doubt and low self-esteem.

This really upset me. I know what it's like to think that you can't achieve something worthwhile, and how debilitating it can be if the thoughts carry on into your twenties and, God forbid, thirties and even forties without being challenged. I knew I had to do something to address the problem.

Whilst working in a college in East London one day, the Principal approached me and asked what could be done to support girls there who were bucking the trend across the UK and not doing as well as might otherwise have been expected. She wanted to use enterprise as a tool to improve both their prospects in terms of their studies, and their futures.

I decided to run one of our usual programme days but make it a girl's only event. I thought it would be an interesting way of seeing what happened both in terms of the attendance rates and the outcomes.

I was blown away.

Not only were we oversubscribed but the group was extraordinarily diverse. The youngest student was sixteen, the oldest seventy-two – back in college to study to become a self-employed bookkeeper. They were from a wide range of backgrounds and academic interests. Some were studying for the usual post-sixteen courses, others for professional qualifications.

What did they all have in common?

A passion. They all wanted to strike out on their own; to devise their own future rather than follow one already laid out for them. But they didn't know how to do it, or they'd tried before and made mistakes so were nervous about trying again.

Some were full of self-doubt; others were confident when it came to their idea but less so about their abilities.

Finally, I realised I'd found an area where I could make a real difference.

The Juno Project was born.

I'm not sure whether this is a good thing to admit or not, but I am one of those people who doesn't plan too much when it comes to how my businesses develop. I love letting things evolve organically and have an innate belief that if it's meant to happen then it will happen. I let my instincts guide me. I will have an idea in my mind of where I need to start, and then I follow not only my thoughts but the ideas that come to me when I meet new people and experience new situations. I knew, in my heart, that this was the next step in my journey – planned or not – where I could make a real difference.

This was an opportunity for me to move into an area I was passionate about. I was determined that I had to do something more concrete to empower and inspire women of all ages to set up their own businesses. Through learning particular skills, they would not only be able to do that – now or in the future if they so wished – but would also be more employable as they would know more about how a business operates.

I was already convinced that women make the best entrepreneurs – they take longer to plan and tend to be more meticulous on the details, thereby negating the risk of failure a little more (although, admittedly, they are more risk averse and often need a real push to get their business up and running). Sorry gents! But the very best bit? The skills that we need to run a business are exactly the same skills we need to be successful in our personal lives.

We all need to be able to negotiate with people; to communicate in a variety of ways; to be relatively literate and numerate; to be organised and good at time management, and to be able to solve problems. The list goes on. But for some reason, a large proportion of these skills aren't picked up either at home or along our educational journey. That means we have huge numbers of young people leaving school and college every year who are hopefully going into the workplace (although if not they're certainly still living their lives), but who aren't resilient, who aren't very confident, and who can't negotiate their wants and needs in a productive manner.

What is the effect?

Back in 2009, whilst studying for my teaching qualification, I spent a month in a women's refuge. I had kept away from men after my marriage ended, too shell-shocked to contemplate being able to trust someone again, and full of self doubt. But finally, after much convincing by my friends, I started dating.

I met someone who seemed perfect and, after some tiny steps, I decided I could trust him. He turned out to be extremely abusive.

It started very subtly – cutting me off from friends – and then became more obvious. One day he told me that I'd never leave him because he'd cut me into tiny pieces and bury me in the garden. Very quickly it escalated to talking to me with his hand around my throat; threatening me. Added to a number of other factors, it became apparent that this was someone who was not only dangerously obsessed with me but also very controlling, and I had to get away.

I was encouraged to contact Women's Aid by some of my college friends and a tutor and, convinced that I was wasting their time, I rang their helpline expecting to be told exactly that.

I was wrong.

Within thirty minutes of the call, my son and I were offered a place in a refuge, having been advised that I was at the upper end of the danger scale – scoring a 13/15 on their advisory test.

When you are in the midst of such a situation you often have no idea of how it is viewed by those looking in. I had been told many times by my friends that I was at risk but I couldn't see it. I knew I was going to move on and away from this man in a few months in any case, and thought I could deal with his behaviour in the meantime. Perhaps I would have done. But perhaps I wouldn't. There's no telling.

I only know that when I walked into the refuge, and the door closed behind me, I had never felt so safe. Ever. Finally there were people who were looking out for me, and trying to help me to move forwards instead of continually moving backwards again.

In that month, I learnt many things about myself, and about my situation. That I could provide financially for my children was not in doubt, but being able to provide emotionally? That was another matter.

I loved them beyond measure and would have protected them with my life, but my own insecurities and belief system were in danger of having a detrimental effect on them. I could see that.

Having been brought up in a dysfunctional family, peppered with abuse and bullying, I had lived my childhood being told that no one loved, liked or wanted me, on a relatively regular basis. That I would achieve nothing.

As a result, I'd grown up thinking that I was worth nothing too, and consequently had little care for my own feelings and welfare – everyone else and what they wanted was much more important than I was. I realised that my marriage had been another carbon copy of every other relationship I'd had before it with men, and with my own family.

I'd followed everyone else's drum, and danced to everyone else's tune. I'd listened to everyone else's opinions on things, and they'd become mine. I'd lived everyone else's life. I had no voice.

In the refuge, I met other women – of all ages – who had had similar experiences. Some had come from very happy childhoods but had lost their way in their teens and been unable to find a path back. Some had just been sweet-talked and before they knew it they were in a situation they couldn't get out of.

Some, like me, came with luggage trolleys worth of baggage and it had affected their way of seeing the world.

But we all had one thing in common. We'd been saved. We'd been given the chance to move forwards onto the paths we should have been travelling on. We could either do that or we could stay where we were.

I chose to move forwards.

My son and I moved out of the refuge; first into a secure hostel to keep us safe a while longer and, when everyone was satisfied that my ex-boyfriend wasn't looking for me, into temporary accommodation. Although I'd had to take a few weeks out from studying whilst everything was up in the air, I finished my studies, winning a coveted award, and landed my first teaching job.

My delight at passing my post-graduate course – having been convinced by various family members that I was stupid, unintelligent and would achieve nothing – was an exquisite feeling.

I remember staring at my certificate, all colours of the rainbow and embossed with gold lettering, and gazing at my name in wonderment. Added to the award certificate, which made me sob when it came in the post (no mean feat in those days, I didn't cry over anything), I truly felt that I'd finally achieved something good. That all the hard years were behind me and that, whilst it wasn't going to be plain sailing ahead, I could cope with anything. Nothing and no one could, or would, faze me any more.

So, fast forward to today. I've been running Operation Enterprise for three years now. As a team, we've worked with countless student entrepreneurs of all ages, helping them to develop their start-ups with our unique programmes. We also work with educational establishments and associated organisations, helping them to develop strategies and businesses for students to participate in whilst learning, as well as support networks and training. I've even been involved in a recent government review of enterprise education, advising on changes that will make a real difference to many young people moving forwards.

The Juno Project is starting to find its feet too. There's a lot of interest in the work we do from all corners of the business world. We are currently developing programmes to work with women's refuges – an obvious cause for me to support – as well as with single mums and girls who have issues around education. We are sourcing corporate funding so that we can offer our courses for free to any woman who wants to come along and are even looking at moving into South America to continue our work.

And from my own point of view – as a female entrepreneur, passionate about supporting anyone who wants to run their own business, but particularly single mums? Well – I've been fortunate not only to be asked to speak at various local and national events, colleges and universities, both about my personal and my entrepreneurial journey, but I've also been invited to meetings at Downing Street to talk about my views on what the government can do to support single mums who want to run their own businesses – as well as being asked to comment on TV about issues of the day relating to female entrepreneurship. None of these things were ever in my original plan when I decided to set up my businesses.

So, you're probably wondering: great story but what does this have to do with me?

One day recently, whilst writing a training programme, I was running through the entrepreneurial traits list that I use with our trainees. I was also turning something over in my mind that related to home.

And I had an epiphany.

I stopped and read the list again. And then I thought back over my journey as a single mum.

I realised that all of the traits that a successful business owner exhibits are those that a single mum needs – and uses – too.

Negotiation, communication, dealing with difficult and complex situations, resilience, balancing the books. You name it. They do it. And so do entrepreneurs.

So why don't more single mums feel they can run their own business? Why do those I've spoken to tell me that they don't have the skills – when they quite plainly do? I know that they would dearly love to make life easier on a financial level, and enjoy the benefits of running a business – and even, perhaps, the challenge. That some feel resigned to working for someone else, and some to not working at all.

So, ladies, I decided that I had to do something about it. I couldn't leave this hanging any more.

I'm going to share all my knowledge and experience with you. From how to set up a business using my tried and tested Start up for Success and WorkIt programmes – and all the hints and tips that we give to the budding business owners that we work with – to the inside info on how I made it all balance and work, as well as the things I did wrong. And there were definitely a few of those...

And it's not just me that's sharing. Along the way, you'll be able to read stories of other single mums and how they've managed to balance not only being a mum but starting up and running a business. And fantastic, heart-warming stories of the children of single mum entrepreneurs, who have been so inspired by their fabulous mums that they've gone on to success themselves.

My greatest wish? That you are so inspired by what you are about to read that you set up your own business too.

Trust me. It's the best thing you will ever do, both for you and your family.

CASE STUDY

Hajra Azim

When 38-year old Hajra's marriage broke down she became a single mum to three girls aged 5, 9 and 16. Since 2012, Hajra has been running a cake-making business, Luv at First Bite, based in Slough, UK. Hajra's business idea came out of doing some local charity work:

I was going through a very emotional time after the separation so to try and get some kind of sanity back into my life I helped raise money for a charity by decorating cakes. I continued baking for family and friends but it wasn't until someone told me that I had the talent to turn my passion into a business that I took control of my life and took steps towards establishing a business. Once I managed to scrape enough money to buy some basic equipment I started baking and decorating cakes and advertised it on Facebook. The biggest challenge I found in starting up a business was trying to convince people that I was serious about what I was doing. This only made me more determined to push this passion of mine and after a few months I managed to establish some clientele. I have gained so much confidence through starting a new business on my own. Being able to do it while looking after my children, as well as being recognised by the local council and coming second place in new small business of the year, are huge successes for me. I've learnt that I can achieve anything that I want to through perseverance and positive thinking. In the future I would like to have my very own coffee/cake shop that I can involve my children in and turn it into a family-run business for generations to come. For me, my business is not about conquering the world.... It's about having conquered my own personal goals.

Website: www.luvatfirstbite.co.uk

Chapter 2: **The challenges**

I love running my own business. There is nothing quite like it. I love that I have taken nothing and made something. That down to my sheer ingenuity, perspiration and bloody-mindedness, I have supported my family for yet another month and will be able to for at least another month to come. Each month. For the foreseeable future and, hopefully, well beyond. That I have only myself to thank for what I have achieved, and only myself to blame if it all goes wrong. That I write my future.

But it's not easy. I'll be very honest about that straight up. No pretence and no over-looking of the facts. I wouldn't want anyone reading this to think that running a business is a walk in the park. It isn't. However, with some support and guidance – and a solid business plan – it is certainly achievable. Many women do run their own businesses and make a great living from them, benefiting from the many positives along the way.

My biggest concern when in the pre start-up stage of my businesses was always cashflow. How I would make ends meet? How would I be sure that I could pay the rent, feed my son, and put petrol in my car to go and earn money? Most of the people I work with in my capacity as a Start-up Coach/Mentor are worried about getting the money together to make it happen.

In my experience, that's the easier of the cashflow problems to overcome. There are many ways that you can find money without having to resort to loans and I will tell you more about these later on in the book. You don't have to get into debt before you've even had a chance to assess in the cold hard light of day whether the business will actually succeed. You can be totally and utterly 100% self-funded with a little resourcefulness and a lot of creative thinking. It's not, by any means, impossible. Believe me, I've done it. Five times! And I've advised others who have gone on to do it themselves too.

In my opinion, the bigger cashflow concern should be focused on bringing in the money each month to keep your head above water; to pay not only your bills but those of the business too, and to be sure that you have a pipeline of monies in stretching far ahead, not just for the next week or two. That's the bit that takes a large part of your work early on and, once you have the structures and processes in place, needs careful monitoring to ensure that it doesn't start to fall apart. The aim is to build on your successes and develop regular revenue streams.

The majority of businesses that fail do so due to cashflow problems. The statistics are quite staggering. Twenty per cent of businesses fold in the first year and, within three years, fifty per cent have closed their doors.

Now I don't want that to put you off but I do want you to go into this with your eyes firmly open. There is a chance your business won't succeed. You may have to go back to the drawing board and start again.

In the UK we have an aversion to the word 'fail'. We see it as a bad thing. As an indictment of ourselves and our abilities. Me? I see it as a platform of growth. We can't achieve if we don't get things wrong. We can't move forwards, onwards and upwards if we don't occasionally fall over. The key is to learn how to dust yourself off, get back up and start again.

We weren't born knowing how to walk, how to speak, how to read. We had to learn. We had to try, fail and try again. Being in business is no different. Be prepared to make mistakes – an awful lot of them – and to learn. If you don't learn, and you don't reflect, you don't get over them.

In this book we'll be examining the importance of reflection, of taking a long, hard look at what has happened – the good and the bad – and how those experiences can be further used in both our business and our personal lives to help us to be the people we want to be, and to have the futures we want to have.

We'll be considering how you can plan not to be one of the businesses that fails; what you need to do to ensure that your fabulous idea has the best chances of success and growth.

I will be sharing my own experiences with you, as will other single mum business owners; showing you what we did to survive the tough financial times and giving you hints and tips to help you do the same. Often, it just takes someone else's sage advice to set off a light bulb moment in your mind, and to help you see a way out of a seemingly impossible situation with no potential solution. I can't imagine a scenario that hasn't been played out many, many times before; that hasn't been looked at, picked over and solved – one way or another. This book will help you to address these issues and find the solution to fit you.

I am fascinated by the reasons that people, male and female, of all ages, give for why they feel they couldn't run a business.

Of course, there will always be people who just don't want to do it. And I respect that. That's a pretty good reason! However, there are plenty of people who do, but they try to convince themselves that they couldn't. Sometimes it's the practical stuff; money, resources, time, knowledge, experience, qualifications. External barriers. Other times it's the internal stuff. The belief that we just don't have what it takes; that someone told us a long time ago we'd never achieve anything and they were right; that we're not clever enough. We don't have the drive and determination to make it happen. The internal barriers.

Often self-fulfilling prophecies.

I am a believer in the fact that anyone can do anything they put their mind to. It doesn't matter what it is, or who it is, it can be done. I imagine that the scientists and inventors who have given us the amazing gadgets and gizmos we now see as an integral part of life thought the same on occasion. They didn't know how they could make their dream happen. But it didn't stop them from carrying on and trying again. And again. And once more for luck. There is evidence to suggest that many of our most talented artists, writers and musicians were written off very early on but they dug deep, found the fortitude they needed and pursued their passions.

Often, those of us who are the most talented are the most belittled.

In my experience of working with student entrepreneurs, the ones who have bags of natural entrepreneurial talent are the ones who have various learning differences, or have dropped out of education because it just didn't suit them. It wasn't what fired them up. It wasn't what they wanted to do.

Now I'm not advocating dropping out of school or college – I'm a big fan of learning but I do understand the frustrations. Education seems to be more about fitting all pegs – square or otherwise – into round holes than delivering what employers, and the real world, really wants. It's widely acknowledged, and who knows when it will change? However, the result is that it puts young people off from learning more, and those who have struggled for whatever reason tend to take on board the often off the cuff and unintended, negative comments from those in positions of authority who should know better. Those who should use their position to enthuse and empower not disenfranchise.

Often these experiences colour our view and perception of what we can do. If someone we've looked up to as a role model and person of worldliness tells us that we are no good, we are more likely to believe it. Even more so if it's a member of our own family.

I've lost count of the number of people who've told me that this was their experience. It was mine too. It does have an impact, and affects confidence, self-esteem and all those other vital strings to our work and personality bow that we need to survive and thrive. It can even stop us from being the person we could be, and turn us into someone we shouldn't be. Someone we don't deserve to be.

We all have these hurdles to overcome – even those who appear to have perfect, storybook lives. Everyone at some point or another has been told something, or has experienced something, that has triggered an incorrect belief in themselves. No one is immune.

Internal barriers are the biggest barriers to overcome. The external stuff is often easily solved and, even if it takes a while, it can eventually be worked out. The internal stuff is trickier. It takes perseverance, determination and courage. It often means stepping out of your comfort zone, and doing things – believing things – you might otherwise never do. But it's worth it. The payback is worth it. Your future is worth it.

As single mums who want to set up a business, there may be a few additional barriers to overcome. There are the usual practical ones that everyone has to face – money, childcare – then the internal ones that we've possibly grown up with. Add in a barrier or two as the result of becoming single mums, and then the most corrosive: the barriers that we face in society.

Much is made, as we already know, of single mums 'sponging off the state' (definitely NOT my words!). According to Gingerbread, twenty-six per cent of UK households are headed by a single parent, and there are two million single parents in total. Sadly, there is still a perception in certain quarters of the UK that being a mum is not a really worthwhile job. And if you are a single mum – well, that's really a no-no. You might as well hold your hands up and admit that all of the ills of the world must be laid at your door because your relationship didn't work out and you are now the carer for your children.

And if you are a single mum on benefits? Well, hang your head in shame!

This makes me very cross. The perception that all single mums on benefits are sitting at home with a 50-inch wide screen TV, nice new car on the driveway, yearly holiday abroad, dripping in gold and going out clubbing once a week, is not only insulting but false.

How anyone can survive a life on benefits is beyond me. For starters, the different levels of benefits are so confusing that I'm surprised anyone can understand them. And they change so often! Different names, different criteria, different levels.

Getting off them to go into work or self-employment is also difficult. I have read countless stories of people who have tried and given up. What does that say about The System? The one that's supposed to be a short term security net for when it's needed and then help you to get back on your feet when you're ready and able?

The other myth around single mums is housing. There seems to be an assumption that all single mums, particularly the young, are queuing up to have reams of children so that they can find themselves a nice little property to nest in. Not all single mums live in social housing, thereby giving housing stability to their kids for as long as they need it. A significant proportion rent from private landlords, where they have little security, and may have to move on a regular basis. Where they can't change anything to make the property a little more homely, not even redecorating because the terms of their lease don't allow it. Where they can't have a small pet, which children learn so much from and is a proven reducer of stress, again because the terms of their lease don't allow it.

Not all single mums stick two fingers up to society at large, laughing at The System with a cigarette in one hand and a large glass of something eye-wateringly alcoholic in the other. The majority are desperate to do more than make ends meet, not to have to rely on benefits in any form (it's incredibly soul destroying to know that you can't support your kids on your own) and to move forwards with their lives in a positive, enriching, and dream-attaining way.

That is the description of single mums that I recognise. They are the single mums that I know. That's me.

I am aware that there are problems around benefits and setting up a business. As I write, there have been a number of articles in the online press regarding those on Job Seekers Allowance wanting to set up a business but not being allowed to use their time to do so. Some have even had their benefits taken away for doing this, not realising that it's not allowed. Any single mum on benefits should go and speak to their local Job Centre about wanting to run a business, and seek out ways that they can be helped.

The scheme that you are most likely to be referred to is the New Enterprise Allowance Scheme. This has been set up purposely to help those who wish to run their own business. Not only are there guaranteed weekly benefit payments for a period of time, but there is also access to a business mentor and then a loan of up to £1000 at the end to fund your business, depending upon its requirements. Of course, I am going to show you why you won't need to take out the loan and how you can fund your business without it, but mentoring is always a great help, particularly when it's free, so take as much advantage of it as you can!

There is a lot of other help out there too at the moment for those who want to set up a business. Along with the New Enterprise Allowance Scheme, the government has introduced a number of other schemes and support networks for budding entrepreneurs, and some are proving to be a great success.

The first to mention is Start up Britain. The website is packed with information, events and offers which may be useful to your business. They operate a bus which tours the UK giving on the spot advice, and the chance to talk to those already running their own businesses. Often a great source of inspiration.

Business Link is another source of information for business owners. Not only is it useful when in the pre start-up and start-up stages, but also as the business grows. There are sections on employing people and exporting, as well as tax and VAT.

The government is also currently offering loans for start-ups via the Start up Loans Company. The age limit has recently been raised and now anyone over the age of 18 can apply. If you are a woman, and interested in taking out a loan – and getting a free mentor – do check out my website which will take you straight through to Start Up Loans HQ or type the following link into your browser:

http://www.startuploans.co.uk/juno

When starting a business, support is vital. As well as government schemes, there are others available that offer free and subsidised mentoring. It is always worth contacting your local Chamber of Commerce to see what help they can offer – for instance, they often run seminars and workshops – as well as attending their networking sessions to meet others in your local area who run their own companies too.

Also to be recommended is contacting your county specific enterprise agency, in addition to the local and county councils, who often run training courses in a wide range of subjects for start-ups as well as more developed businesses. Some industries have their own networking groups, likely to be more plentiful in more urban areas, and there are also gender specific business networking groups. Local colleges and universities may also offer free courses and support.

From the point of view of being a mum, or a single mum, who is running a business or out working, there are online groups that you can join; some of these are now developing physical networking groups. Try groups like Gingerbread and MumpreneurUK.

However, despite the help and support being offered, it can sometimes feel as though you are very alone, both as a single mum and a solo start-up entrepreneur. Both jobs can be isolating, as well as tiring. Both can also be immensely rewarding.

Take the leap. Join me on one of the most rewarding journeys you will take.

CASE STUDY

Conan is 26 and is a test engineer for one of Ireland's largest communication companies. He is based in Dublin, Ireland.

I can remember from back when my mum's business was just a thought. I have a sense of pride that my Mam is a successful business owner. It has given her independence; she no longer has to work for someone else and is her own boss. She now works at something that she has a genuine interest in, which I feel makes a huge different to the attitude you have towards your job. My mum has taught me a great work ethic, she has taught me the value of life and to make the most of what you have. I want to upskill and progress my career in communications, to be able to provide a comfortable and happy life for my family. The attitude I have today was instilled in me by my Mam from a young age, so in that way, she has inspired me.

Chapter 3: **The positives**

I must be honest and say that I am a bit of a small business-aholic. I love everything about planning, starting up and running a business. There really is nothing that compares, certainly not when it comes to work. I'm the kind of person who loves a challenge; who likes to take an idea and see where it goes – who likes to test herself.

But I wasn't always like that.

I had a difficult childhood and upbringing. It left me doubting myself and my abilities. Everyone made my decisions for me – I was often told I had no opinion – and I didn't feel in control of my life.

It took until my marriage broke down, and then a little longer after when I was in a women's refuge, for me to really start getting a handle on who I was and what I could do. I suddenly realised that I could do anything! That there were no boundaries, only those I put around myself. That if I wanted to try something I could, and no one could tell me otherwise.

I think that we all come to a point in our lives when we suddenly realise that what other people think doesn't matter. That it's only our feelings and beliefs that should dictate what we do. Other people shouldn't be allowed to make our decisions on our behalf. It's a landmark when we reach it, and often it comes with age.

And what a revelation it is.

I have found working for other people quite difficult. Secretly I think I may not be the best of employees. I learn really quickly, so get bored very easily. I then want to move on to other things and, if I can't, I become disillusioned and start metaphorically kicking at the tyres, looking for something more interesting. That means most of my jobs have only lasted for around a year or so.

I have a very short attention span. If you can't keep me interested then I can guarantee my mind will wander, and that's when the trouble will start. I am very adept at assessing business situations swiftly and succinctly. I can see how things can be done more quickly, more efficiently and more effectively. This means that I can be perceived as a bit of a boat rocker. I don't mean to be, far from it, but I can't help but observe. And then speak. That gets you into trouble too.

I am also a little on the outspoken side – as you may have guessed! I can stay silent for a while but eventually my sense of injustice can't keep quiet any more and it raises its head.

In all honesty, I don't think I'm a team player. I love working with other people, absolutely love it, but at heart I'm a one-woman band. I operate best on my own, working off my ingenuity and energy. I have a bit of a 'spider brain' so I'll see patterns that others might not and, given that I also use my intuition, I am the one who will take a risk in a work environment. I know it will work and don't think I need to justify myself. Of course, bosses don't see things the same way. I need to be trusted and allowed to do my thing. Bosses need to see a track record first; they need you to earn their trust. I don't have time for that. If you're employing me to do a job I need to get up at it and on it.

You can see why I'm not a great employee. I don't think I have the mindset nor the personality for it. Over the years, particularly when money has been tight, I've wished I had. How much easier it might have been to find a nicely paid job with a bit of a challenge, working with a group of people I liked.

But no. I could do it for a few months but eventually I'd be bored. And then the whole cycle would start again.

Running my own business really works for me. The whole success and failure rests on my shoulders and my shoulders alone. It's down to me which route it takes. It's down to me to ensure that I make the correct decisions, and put the right processes in place so that I don't find myself in a position where the business might fall over. And as it grows, it's down to me to find the right people to manage it and ensure its long-term survival.

That means that I can take the risks if my instinct tells me to. That I can change the way things are run if I feel they need to be changed. That I can pursue new revenue streams and potential diversifications if the business case is strong enough. I can give myself interesting things to do to keep me motivated when I've done lots of the not so interesting things. I can let my imagination run wild and indulge my passions. I can set ridiculously challenging targets and then bust a gut reaching them. And if I don't, who is going to be the loser?

Me.
Every time, it's going to be me.

And I can live with that. Because the positives are so many.

Apart from the freedom and the autonomy in my work environment, I also get the freedom to dictate my own working hours and patterns. I'm responsible for my diary, so if I want to take a day off I can. If I want to take things easy one day and work at a slower pace, then I can. If I need to do something at home then I can. There's no boss to have to beg to. I'm my own boss.

Of course, there's always work to catch up with, but that's the recognised pay off. Want a day off – work for another two to catch up (or so it feels sometimes!). As the business grows I can delegate work out to other people but at the moment it's me working a large proportion of the time. But that's changing fast.

People set up businesses for all kinds of reasons. Some have the same desires as I did – flexible hours and the ability to earn more than they could working for someone else. Others are just looking for an extra part-time income, or to indulge a passion and earn some money whilst doing so. I know of lots of people who do that – fantastically talented craftspeople, cake decorators, pet sitters, fitness instructors etc.

When I started my first business on my own, lack of childcare provision was the main driver. Not only was it difficult to actually find someone local to me who could look after my son before and after school – affordability was of secondary relevance if there was no-one to do it – but to find something suitable through the holiday periods too? It appeared that I was asking for the impossible. I quickly figured out that if I worked for myself, I could work around my son – get up really early to do the admin stuff, make calls when he was at school, and catch up on more admin when he went to bed – and I'd juggle my time through the holidays.

And it worked!

Not only could I still earn a living but my son and I got to spend more time together. I could be at home with him when he finished school, whereas before I was lucky if I got an hour with him before he went to bed. I could oversee homework, rather than asking the childminder to do it for me and, crucially, I managed to help him with his emotional worries about his father and I splitting up too. That was the part that was having the most impact on him, and the thing that concerned me most of all. So we both benefited.

Of course, being at home more meant that I could also be around for the other household chores and issues that we all need to address. I could put a load in the washing machine and then get on with some work; prepare supper at lunchtime and pop it in the oven in between calls or whatever else was happening; be at home, without losing a day's pay, if I needed to be.

When you are a working single mum with multiple plates to spin, having that kind of flexibility is invaluable. Being able to do home stuff and work stuff at the same time is the stuff of dreams! It uses up some of the dead business time (everyone has a little here and there, don't believe them when they say otherwise) and enables you to turn it into live home time and vice versa. You can't achieve that if you work for someone.

Of course one of the big talking points of the moment, and one that crops up on a regular basis, is that of earning potential. It is no secret that women earn, on average, nineteen per cent less than men when working in equivalent roles. There are lots of debates as to why but, in my opinion, no amount of talking is going to solve the problem. Rightly or wrongly. I'd rather leave the experts to debate the issue and get on with earning as much as I can – and if it's more than my male counterpart then so much the better. I'm not hung up on the pay gap battle; I completely understand women's frustrations and their anger but I don't shout about it. I fight it on the ground, on my ground, by getting on with running my business. I'm lucky that I don't have to confront it on a daily basis; that I don't have to argue my point. Believe me, I've been there – I've worked in roles where my male colleague earned a basic salary of fifteen per cent more than I did for spurious reasons which I've still never understood, and were explained to me by my FEMALE boss who made the salary decisions. But I've taken it in my stride. I knew that, at some point, I would be earning far more than they would ever be able to count. And I'd have a much nicer lifestyle too. (Just between us, I've some way to go yet but don't tell them that ...)

Running my own business means that, not only do I determine what I earn but, if I want to give myself a pay rise and I believe the business can sustain it, then I can do whatever I like. Of course, there are some months when I can take very little from the businesses (they are still very young after all), but overall I have a much higher earning potential than I ever would have done as an employee. Even comparing my teachers' salary of three years ago with my self-employed salary of today shows an eye watering difference.

It also means that I can plan to achieve the goals I have set for myself and can earn the money I need to support both myself and my family; that I can finally end up in a position where I have my own property – not a rented one – and can help my children to buy their own properties too. I would never have been able to achieve that as an employee, certainly not at my age, and would probably have been resigned to renting forever. Moving whenever my landlord wanted his/her property back. Not knowing whether the house I lived in would be the one I could relax in and enjoy, or would have to give back. Worrying about paying rent into my nineties (I plan to live to at least one hundred years old – still so much to achieve!).

For me, this is the biggest reason I run my own business. I simply can't accept that I have owned my own properties in the past but won't again. That I had control over where I lived, and how I lived, but won't again.

I am absolutely determined that I will get back to being a home owner, whatever it takes, and I will therefore work more hours in a day than exist, use up more brain cells than I have in my tiny mind by devising new ideas and creating new projects, and travel more miles than is humanly possible – all in the name of my own dream.

Oh, and be a mum too.

I also want economic independence. A tall order, I know, but it's what really drives me now. One of the biggest hurdles I had to overcome when I became a single mum was going back to a solitary income but with two, often three, mouths to feed. No maintenance payments – just my salary.

I must be honest and say that I have moments when I envy those in a relationship. They have the things I really desire in life; companionship, solidarity, friendship, love and support – a family unit – and, of course, the really practical bit; two incomes. Life is instantly easier. Less pressured.

But I made a decision when my husband and I split up that I was never going to rely on another person financially again. Ever. I didn't care what it took but I would never again put myself in the position of giving everything, sharing everything, losing everything and having to start again from scratch, whilst they walked away able to begin again much more quickly than I was. Never again was I going to give someone the chance to knock me down and, potentially, cripple me financially. Never again was I going to be that vulnerable.

It has taken me a very long time to get to a point of relative financial security – nine years – and I'm not there yet but I'm certainly closer than I have been. My ex left me with debts and financial obligations that he point blank refused to honour, abandoning me to do so on my own. It was an incredibly difficult time to work through and I am reminded of the horror every so often. It fills me with dread, gives me occasional nightmares, and has definitely affected my views on money and security.

Now, I won't have been the only single mum to find herself in this position and I have no doubt that other women will follow in exactly the same footsteps – not because they are in that situation through choice, or don't listen to those of us who have been around the block a few times, but due to circumstance. Being responsible for your own financial destiny is so empowering. Knowing that you are the one who brings in the money, and that you don't need to rely on anyone else is such a gift. For some it is through employment; for others like me it's through self-employment. However you do it, just do it. The sense of achievement is overwhelming. Knowing that you control the financial aspect of your life is simply smile-making.

Of course, with all this comes a big increase in self-esteem. Feeling more in control; more able to do what you want without someone telling you that you can't or putting obstacles in your way.

Coming from a place where your confidence and self-esteem have likely taken a bit of a battering for whatever reason, planning and then starting your own business gives you a brilliant chance to start putting yourself together. To take a close, in-depth look at how talented and resourceful you are and to be proud of what you can achieve. To accept that, whilst you can't do everything, you can do something and this is your chance to do it and to shine. To learn that hurdles are made to be jumped over not refused, and that they are merely a blip in life's rich journey.

When you put yourself in new or difficult situations, you quickly learn just what you are made of. More often than not, you find that you are made of the stuff that gets you through, not the stuff that leaves you stuck. And a little bit of you is proud of the stuff of which you are made. So next time, you try something a little more difficult, because last time you found you could cope. And, once more, you find your stuff does you proud. So you try again. Maybe this next time it doesn't quite go your way because, let's face it, sometimes that's what happens. But after a bit of a panic perhaps – you're allowed – you remember how well you have bounced back, and how your stuff has seen you right so far. So you stop panicking and carry on trying.

After a few rounds of the success and setback cycle, you realise that you can do whatever you set your mind to. And that the people around you are right. You're amazing. In fact, you're bloody marvellous (although, secretly, you may not accept that for some time to come but, take it from me, you should). So you keep trying. And you keep learning. And when it goes wrong, you smile and pick yourself up and carry on. Because who cares? Who really cares that it went wrong? No one. Do you know why?

We all get it wrong every so often. To get it right, we have to get it wrong. I'm from the school that would rather throw myself in the deep end straight away and get it wrong early on – get the mistakes out of the way – than umm and ahh about doing something, think about it, think a bit more, and then find that I've thought so much that the opportunity has either long gone or I've gone off the idea altogether.

Seize the moment. Prove to yourself that you can do what you set your mind to, and see just how quickly your self-esteem soars.

CASE STUDY

Raphael Bignall

Raphael, 26, works as a supervisor in a retail store in Radstock, UK, but aspires to become a computer game designer.

As a teenager I remember my mum being a Virtual PA working from home, although I'm not sure I understood what she was doing. I liked that she was home more than when she was working as an employee. Mum has always told me to do my own thing, to find what I love and follow it. When I left drama school because I knew I didn't want to do it anymore there was no big argument or shake down with mum, she just asked me what else I wanted to do and we looked at the possibilities. In the future I want to run my own business designing computer games and being involved in the development of future technologies. Mum has encouraged me to see that work life does not have to be nine-to-five, in an office or shop; there are other choices. She has shown me that success is accomplishing what you want for yourself.

Chapter 4: Setting up a business – 'You'

A common misconception is that a business is built purely upon a good idea, and that's all that's needed. It is, of course, true that a business needs a good idea but it also needs someone good to develop it. A business is as much about you as it is your idea. You can have the best business idea in the world but if you don't have the skills or the mindset to develop it, then the idea won't take off. You can be the most enterprising person in the world but if you don't have well thought through and marketable ideas, then you will struggle to make a success of them, even given your undoubted skills.

Entrepreneurs like to think that they are good at everything, even the things that they aren't so good at. That's probably not such a surprise, given that they are extremely optimistic and positive people, but at some point or another it becomes obvious that they need help with a particular skill or business area, and those who are wise enough will secure that help – enabling their business to move forwards in a positive manner. Not being aware of your strengths and weaknesses is an elementary business mistake, so when you start planning a business it's one of the first things you should consider:

What can I do?

What can't I do?

And if I can't do it – who can I find who can?

Entrepreneurial skills

There are a group of skills that are widely accepted as those that an entrepreneur needs, or exhibits, in their working lives. When you look at the list, you will see that we all need these skills on a personal level too – we all need to be able to negotiate, to communicate, and to calculate basic budgets etc – so, in theory, there shouldn't be anything that will take you very far out of your comfort zone.

However, as I have pointed out, there will be some that you already know are not strong points, so you will need to make a note of these and decide how you will cover them off before launching your business.

Creative	Persuasive
Good communicator	Listens to their gut feeling (intuition)
Good negotiator	Copes with uncertainty and complexity
Confident	Builds trust with others
Can present information	Resilient
Can present themselves	Literate
Focused	Numerate
Independent	Risk taker
Problem solver	

As I go through the list, you will see that the skills are heavily interlinked; that one often relies upon another. So they shouldn't be seen as separate, but rather as a package that gives us the rounded entrepreneurial nature we require to set up our own business.

Creative

When I talk about being creative, I don't mean being good at art and crafts (which is lucky as I need to label anything I draw...). I mean creativity in its much broader sense. Doing things in a creative way, thinking in a creative way, i.e. not just using a very narrow set of guidelines, or doing things in a way you've always done them. You need to think 'outside the box' – a dreadful phrase but it does hit the nail on the head.

Being creative as an entrepreneur is all about letting your mind run free, coming up with all kinds of solutions and scenarios. It's not ruling things out before you've even had a chance to plan them, let alone try them. It's accepting that setting up a business is a step into an unknown world; one where there are no guarantees and few guidelines. Therefore, thinking in a creative way is a really positive and helpful thing – it helps you to tackle problems and to solve them much more easily than using the same old same old. Of course there is a place for the same old same old but as an entrepreneur, there is more of a place for thinking creatively.

Good communicator

In all areas of life, in every one you can possibly imagine, it's accepted that communication is important. None more so than when running a business, for not only are you communicating yourself, but you are also communicating on behalf of your company.

We communicate in a variety of different ways and each one has to be considered and thought through in a business context.

Verbal

Forty-five per cent of all communication is verbal.

When we talk to someone, in any situation, we must be sure that what we say is communicated clearly. There is much research around regional accents and what we assume from them, particularly in business. For me, accents are no issue – it's how we speak that's important. Clearly, slowly and professionally. Consider what you are saying, practise the more important 'speeches' beforehand (including new business pitches and general product/service information), and always speak with a smile. People can hear it in your voice, particularly on the telephone and it makes them more at ease.

I tend to talk quite quickly, especially when I get excited about something, and occasionally have had to consciously slow myself down. When clients get to know me they appreciate that it's all part of the 'Ali Experience', but initially it can be a little overwhelming. It's a really good idea to slow down, take your time over what you are saying, and pace yourself. After all, you need to get your points across clearly and concisely and no amount of rushing will allow you to do that. The last thing you want is for someone to tell you they didn't quite hear what you said, and ask you to repeat yourself. It's happened to me a few times, and it makes for an awkward moment.

Speaking in a professional manner is also vitally important. When someone meets you for the first time they take everything on board. They also listen carefully to what you say, and judge you on it. If you swear liberally and rubbish your competitors, what does that say about you? What does it say about your potential client? The one who's likely to have made the decision to use one of your competitors? To them, it says that you think they are of poor judgement and need educating. That's not the way to get a new client.

If you swear, it's an instant turn off. Irrespective of whether you are working in a roughty-toughty world, promoting your business to a client who swears like a trooper or not, it is not professional to do the same. Businesses need to have standards. High standards. Their owners need to promote those high standards at every opportunity. Swearing does not do that.

Practise your company introduction with a friend. Hone it down until not only are you word perfect but you can say it in only a few minutes. One of the biggest mistakes we make when first setting up a business – and we've all done it – is that our passion for what we are doing overtakes us and we speak for far too long. A few minutes is more than enough to say what you have to say and get on with booking a new client. Not send them to sleep.

Listening

'We have two ears and one mouth – and should use them in that proportion.' A very apt saying and never more so than in business. One of the elementary mistakes that people new to sales, and nervous of sales, make is that of talking too much and not listening enough. Listening is the key to making a sale, and a much underrated skill.

I have worked in sales for over thirty years and it took me a long time to learn to listen properly. But doing it properly yields such great results and, in fact, a potential pipeline of extra sales as you find out that your client not only wants the product/service you are selling, but they then merrily tell you of other things they may require too. If you'd been busy talking and not so busy listening, or busy thinking about what you were going to say next and not busy listening, you'd have missed the clues.

I always take a pen and paper to every meeting, and I put them in front of me. Sometimes, very rarely, I don't use them but more often than not I do. They are a physical reminder to me in that meeting to listen, to take notes, and to follow up on what I promise to do when I'm back in the office. To show my customer that I care about their business as much as they do.

Clients value being listened to, and are more likely to use a company that makes them feel as though their business is important through having listened to their requirements. The client is the star of the meeting after all. That's who you've come to see. So do them the courtesy of listening to what they have to say.

Listening skills are very easy to improve. We all have them, we just don't use them. Practise on a friend. Have a conversation but let them do all the talking, and then repeat back what you've heard. You'll be surprised what other communication skills you might also improve whilst you're at it.

Non-verbal

Fifty-five per cent of all communication is non-verbal.

It takes seven seconds for us to make a first impression. That means it takes seven seconds for someone to gain a first impression of us. That's not much time for us to get it right. So how can we make sure that first impression is what we want it to be?

When you first meet someone in a formal setting, what do you do? Do you grab at their hand, hold it in a half-hearted way, look down and mumble a few words? Or do you confidently smile, hold your hand outstretched to meet theirs, clasp it firmly, look them in the eyes and introduce yourself?

The latter is definitely preferable!

I understand that this is one of the hardest things for people to do, for it involves confidence and we don't all have bags of that. However, I can guarantee you that doing it correctly will give you the confidence you need to get it right the next time, and the next time.

Smiling is probably one of the most important non-verbal keys you can use. What do we assume from a smile? What do we see and how does it make us feel? And how does it make us feel to smile? It all adds up to the same thing – confidence. Smiling makes us look, and feel, confident. It also makes us look approachable and friendly, which is what we want potential clients to think we are. After all, not only is it true of course, but clients would much prefer to work with someone who has a smile on their face than one who doesn't – particularly in a business area where there is a close customer-business owner interaction. Wouldn't we all?!

We also give a lot away via our body language. How we stand, how we sit, how we hold and carry ourselves. If we sit talking to someone in a business meeting but our eyes are constantly flitting around the room – what does that say about us? If we are presenting information about our company but we are clicking the top of a pen on and off – what does that say about us? More importantly, what does it potentially say about the information we are giving to our client? What might they think? Clicking the top of a pen could signify nerves, which could in turn signify that we aren't necessarily telling the truth. So what does that suggest about our products or services? Now that might not be the case but how is the client to know? Clients will act on what they observe.

I must be honest and admit that I am a bit of a fiddler generally. Although I've learned to curtail my compulsion to take pen lids on and off in meetings, or to twist in my seat and look around the room, it is still a challenge some days. I find formal, corporate-style meetings the trickiest things to deal with. Those of us who are dyspraxic may find this to be a problem more than most for a variety of reasons.

So how have I managed it? Well, the trick is to do something less obvious than clicking pens and twisting in your chair. I now always have a pen in my hand. Always. Whatever I am doing. For some reason it makes that part of my brain that is far too active, less so. I make sure it isn't one with a clicky top (I WILL click it) or a removable lid (I WILL keep putting the lid on and then taking it off), and I just keep it in my hand. Sometimes I know that I twirl it through my fingers, a little like a drum majorette with a baton, but it's the best I can manage!

If you have this problem too, then you need to find something relatively innocuous to occupy your hands. Your mind should be occupied with the meeting, and the intricacies of what is being discussed – particularly as it is your business and you have more than a vested interest – but your hands could well be another matter.

Other forms of communication include our dress sense, the way we present ourselves generally and the marketing of our company – all of which we will look at over the course of this book.

Good negotiator

How many times have you found yourself negotiating with your kids – usually over bedtimes, or playing outside for another thirty minutes – and suddenly realised that you are supposed to be the one in charge, telling them what to do not having them try to convince you otherwise? Well, you aren't alone! However, be glad! Negotiation skills are vital for running a business.

Dealing with clients, suppliers and staff requires a level of negotiating expertise, and it's always one of the skills at the top of most people's list when I ask, 'Which one of the skills on this list do you think you are least good at?'

I guess I shouldn't be surprised. Negotiation is seen as a sales technique and, given that most people cower whenever I mention the dreaded S word, it is to be expected. However, when I then start giving examples of when we have all used negotiation skills in our every day lives, the black cloud sitting on the forehead starts to break and the penny drops.

We all negotiate on a regular basis but just don't tend to realise it.

Key tips for negotiation? Know what you want from the deal, and go in hard. Start at the upper end of what you want. Be prepared to drop down a bit – so don't expect to get everything you ask for – but know your lowest limit. And stick to it! Negotiate down, not up.

We've all had experiences of bad negotiations – I still cringe when I remember some of the truly dreadful deals I've been a party to, including one recently (yes, I still make mistakes!). But I no longer lose sleep over it. My best advice is to chalk it up to experience and move on, although it's easy to let a bad negotiation knock your confidence. Don't. We all do it. We will all continue to do it; but hopefully less often, and it's a rite of business passage. After all, what would you have to discuss over a glass of wine with a friend otherwise?!

Confident

Our confidence can be very easily knocked. One minute we are 'up' and feeling very positive, yet it only takes one ill-judged comment or unkind criticism and we feel less sure of ourselves. A few more piled on top, and before we know where we are we're convinced that we just can't achieve anything. I know. I've been there.

When you grow up being told that people don't want you, that you won't achieve much, it stays with you. It's always been at the back of my mind and coloured so much of what I've done and how I see myself. Until recently that is.

Having spent a month in a women's refuge, I suddenly realised that I had to change. That I couldn't spend my life letting other people's opinions of themselves, which they then transferred onto me, ruin my opinion of me. My perception of what I could be. The only person who could take charge and make that change was me. So I did.

Now, I'm not saying it was easy, it was far from it. But if I wanted to move forwards and do something positive – something special – with my life, then I knew I had to let the past go, and move on to the future.

I found that running a business, and dealing with all of its inherent challenges, actually improved my confidence. Being seen as an expert by clients, purely for using my knowledge, skills and talents to help them; being asked to speak on particular topics because of my knowledge, skills and talents, and being congratulated on my successes, all boosted my confidence. I suddenly realised that if people from a wide spectrum of backgrounds and ages thought I was good at what I did, then I must be. And, added to my success in running my business and overcoming the cashflow problems, the staffing issues, and the other things that crop up on a regular basis – that meant that actually I was quite good at something. So I became more confident.

Confidence is contagious. If you feel confident, you look confident, and when you then talk in a business scenario people are enthused by your confidence. If it's a sales meeting, it therefore follows that they are going to be confident in you and your company.

Sometimes you have to develop a second persona in order to achieve this. For me, I have Professional Ali and Personal Ali. Professional Ali is confident, dynamic, motivated and driven; a bit of a risk junkie. She has opinions on things and, when the setting is right, she's happy to share them. She has that pizzazz that people are drawn to. She's not afraid.

Personal Ali is a little quieter, not so confident, less riddled with self-doubt than she used to be, and getting there more each day. She will say what she thinks, but only in the right company, and dislikes confrontation intensely to the point where she will actively run in the opposite direction if necessary. She isn't particularly afraid but she isn't keen to take risks.

I use Professional Ali all the time at work, and I channel the more feminine qualities through from Personal Ali when the need arises. At home, I sometimes wish I was more like Professional Ali, and am slowly learning how to integrate her positive qualities without it seeming as though I am always in work mode to my kids. And to me. It's good to switch off!

Try doing the same. We all have slightly different work and personal personas; see if you can beef up the work one, thereby projecting a level of confidence, without scaring clients half to death of course...

Can present information

You may be surprised to see that I have deliberately separated presentation skills into two sections – presenting information, and presenting yourself.

It's a given that we will have to present information when running a business, but people often forget that we are also presenting ourselves – and it's in this area that mistakes can be easily made.

When I work with students who want to start up a business and I ask them how they can present information, they are often very clued up. They know that the use of technology is expected for formal presentations – some use PowerPoint, others have gravitated to Prezi. It's entirely their preference. They know that you need to know your audience, what will appeal to them and how to reach them with what you have to say; and they know that speaking clearly and articulately, pausing for breath occasionally, and asking if there are any questions are key points. And that's all great.

However, in a less formal situation where there is just you and your potential client, a glossy brochure and sleek, short, verbal presentation may well be enough. For instance, if you are running a beauty salon you aren't going to insist on delivering a fifteen-minute Powerpoint presentation to each potential new client who walks through the door. That would be overkill. But a brochure, with a brief informative chat and perhaps a tour of the salon, would be perfect.

It's all about your audience. What would suit one business wouldn't necessarily suit another. This is an area in which you can do some research and decide how you will approach clients, and how you can show your company off to its best.

Presenting yourself

Entrepreneurs, and anyone setting up a business or working on a freelance basis, need to know how to present themselves. It's a non-negotiable. You are the face of your work. Meeting you may well be the first opportunity that your client has had to consider your company and what it stands for, although it must be said that technology is so far advanced these days that a client may well have checked out your website, Twitter, Facebook, Instagram, LinkedIn and other social media marketing outlets beforehand – so be aware! However, it is you that the client will buy so it's imperative that you present yourself perfectly.

Before we look at anything else, let's look at you. What would you wear for a client meeting? Most people would opt for the default business attire, but if your business is in creative media or construction for instance, then you would probably be more casual. Just a word of warning for those in construction – casual doesn't mean covered in paint, sawdust or with holes in your jeans. I've run two construction businesses myself, so I know!

For those with businesses that require uniforms – hair, beauty, vehicle mainte-nance, for example – that's probably just how your client will expect to see you dressed.

Once you've sorted out what you will wear, the next thing to consider is how you greet your client. We've mentioned before about non-verbal communication and how important it is to show your positivity through your body language. Well, presenting yourself is an extension of that.

When you meet someone for the first time, the two things you should have signed off are how you will shake their hand and how you will look at them. I have heard many quotes about how these are the markers of someone you can trust, and I can certainly say that my experience backs this up. I have shaken many a wet fish hand and, quite frankly, it's off-putting at best, and makes me want to rush off and scrub my hand with bleach at worst. A handshake is so important. Whilst it should be firm – no loosely held fingers, no half-hearted attempt at shaking, or grabbing of one finger (all of which I have personally experienced) – and conducted with the right hand not the left, it shouldn't be so firm as to leave the 'shakee' with a loss of sensation in their hand and a bright purple bruise.

The best advice I can give you is to practise. Practise on friends and family (and if they need some help with their own handshake, point it out). And keep practis-ing. I can't stress enough how vital it is to get a handshake right.

Thinking about how you will look at someone when you first meet them might seem like a rather trite thing for me to point out, but I have a reason. Many is the time I have met someone – both as a salesperson and potential customer – and they can't make eye contact with me. They will look anywhere and everywhere except at me. To the side, above my head, at their feet, at their hand. None of those are where my eyes are and it is more than a little off-putting. It doesn't fill me with confidence.

Being able to look someone full square in the eye when you meet them is so important. We are visual. We take a lot of our clues about a person from the way they respond when we look at them and they look at us. And you need that contact to then progress a business meeting into, hopefully, a long term, fruitful business relationship.

There's no need to get into a staring competition. We're not talking about looking at someone until they can't help but look away, but it is important to look someone in the eye, and to keep eye contact on a regular basis throughout your meeting. Have a think back to when someone has avoided eye contact with you – how did it make you feel? What were you tempted to do, or not do? These aren't the impressions you want someone to have of you.

So an initial meeting involves smiling, shaking hands with a firm handshake and looking your potential client in the eye, whilst speaking clearly. It's not difficult to achieve, but can take some practice.

Something to consider: in different cultures there are different accepted business traditions. If you are going to be running your business in a multi-cultural environment – and that is the majority of us these days – please take the time to research these topics in a bit more detail.

So, your introduction went well, and you are sitting down with your potential client. What else do you need to consider?

What have you brought with you? Pen? Paper? Brochures? Business cards? Business cards are the first thing you should take out and give to your potential client. It's almost like a ritual. Make sure they are kept in a safe place in your bag or briefcase so that they aren't worn and dog-eared by the time you give them to your client. Not a great first impression. I always carry business cards with me everywhere I go. You never know when you might meet someone you want to make contact with, or where!

Pen and paper. Now call me old-fashioned but, as mentioned, I still use both of these in meetings, and carry them wherever I go. I appreciate that those of you who are younger and more technologically savvy will be quite happy making notes on a laptop or tablet – although you should be aware that there may not be space, in a more formal meeting, for you to use a bulky item. You may have to use your lap. However, there is still a use for the pen. I'm hoping that your meeting goes so well that your potential client becomes your new client – and you want them to sign a contract, which, of course, you have with you. But you have no pen? Not very professional. Always take one with you.

Brochures are always useful to give out in meetings. Leaving something behind for your client to read at a later date is a great marketing tool, and it ensures that your number and contact details are always to hand should they decide they want to get in touch.

Focused

If you want to be successful, at anything, you have to be focused. You have to be conscious of what you want to achieve, how you are going to do it, and what you will need to get there. The end goal has to be marked up and worked towards

However, it's also very easy to lose focus, particularly – ironically – when things are going well. Some of us are more prone to it than others. We work incredibly hard towards something we want, overcome all sorts of hurdles and obstacles and then, when we successfully reach the first stage of our goal, we lose our concentration in the celebrations. We forget the urgency to why we were doing what we were doing because we've succeeded. And it can sometimes be quite hard to get back on track.

I wouldn't be too hard on yourself if you are one of those people. Being focused can be difficult, and it's not something that comes easily to us all. A tip that I can offer here is that I don't keep what I want to achieve in my head – I write it down. And then I plan out what I need to do to get there; all of the stages, and the in between steps too. Then I draw up an End Goal. The 'What Will My Achievement Mean To Me' list. And I pin it at the top of my stages plan. That way if I lose focus one day, I can look at my diagram and what I will get from achieving my goals; and I'm reminded of what I am aiming for, and what I need to do next to get there. We can't all be super-focused, and neither should we be. It's our differences that make us great! But we can try to plug the gaps in advance of when we have a not-so-focused day. Thinking ahead makes us great too.

Independent

As a single mum, you will have already learned the value of independence; of being able to make your own decisions without recourse to someone else (often there is no one else!), and that's a vital part of being a business owner too. Particularly if you are a solo entrepreneur.

I run both my businesses on my own. Every decision is down to me, and me alone. I have no one else to ask for their opinion on a day to day basis and so the choices I make are solely down to me. They are completely my responsibility.

Now, not everyone is comfortable with this. Some people aren't entirely happy with making a decision unless they have been able to ask advice from others first – and I completely understand that. However, to run a business you have to be able to make quick and effective decisions, sometimes on the spot, and often without being able to ask anyone their opinion. This is where the skill of being independent comes in.

You also have to be comfortable striking out on your own, sometimes into an area of uncharted water so to speak, and seeing where it takes you. Not relying on others.

Part of the reason that I set up my businesses on my own (and I know I am far from alone in this) is that I love being independent. I love making my own decisions and not having to rely on anyone. I love the freedom it gives me and I have no problem with the fact that if I make a wrong decision, it's down to me. There is no one else to blame.

Being independent also relies heavily on confidence. You are unlikely to want to strike out on your own in something if you have no confidence in your ability to do it successfully. Therefore planning is vital. It gives you the confidence in what you are about to try, to then do it alone.

Of course, you don't have to do everything in a business on your own – far from it – and there are many people who set up businesses with partners. But be prepared that at points along your entrepreneurial journey, independence will be a skill you will draw upon again and again.

Problem solver

If you like solving problems, then you will love running your own business. Problems can be a bit like buses; you wait ages for one and then three come along at the same time. Being an entrepreneur yields an unpredictable lifestyle – and problem solving is a very useful skill. Just as it is when you are a single mum!

As we've seen with other skills, not everyone finds problem solving easy. However, we all problem solve on a daily basis so I think that some people just don't realise they are already doing it! And, again, it links in heavily with confidence.

So if you are one of those people who throws their hands up in the air and decries their problem solving abilities on the basis that they just aren't very good – here are a few pointers on improving:

1. Identify the problem. Sometimes we look at the big picture and don't drill down to the real problem underneath.

2. Mind map some potential solutions. There is rarely one solution to a problem, so let your mind go wild and come up with all the possible answers there may be. Do a bit of creative thinking. And if you can involve others, so much the better.

3. Evaluate your solutions. Think about the impact the solution would have on your overall goal, and how difficult the solution might be to implement. Ideally, you would like high-impact and low-difficulty answers.

4. Do it! Plan and then implement your solution. And do it well. You've spent all this time considering the problem; don't get the Do It bit wrong.

5. Reflect. An underrated and underused skill. Look at the good and the bad, and how you can improve next time.

Persuasive

Now we get a bit controversial. Persuasiveness is a really useful skill when setting up/running a business, for very obvious reasons. It's important that you are able to convince – or persuade – someone that they should use and support your company, employing a variety of mediums. I tend to go a step further and use the word 'manipulate' – not just because I like being a bit controversial (it makes for great discussions) but also because, if we're going to get to the bottom of some of the more difficult to accept skills, then that's sometimes a good way to do it.

I don't know why it is that people get het up over the idea of being persuasive. I wonder whether they see it as a bad thing. In terms of the women I work with, perhaps it's seen as something that girls don't do. That to be persuasive means using our feminine wiles. Ladies, you couldn't be further from the truth if that's the case.

Persuasiveness sits in the sales group of skills, along with negotiation and presentation abilities. It's a bona fide, essential technique that business owners engage in countless times over the course of an average week. From the company marketing, to dealing with banks and financiers, staff, suppliers and clients – persuasiveness is at the heart of a lot of business activities.

And single mums use persuasion too! It may not be in exactly the same circumstances as an entrepreneur (not with staff or suppliers, for instance), but I can guarantee it's in use on a regular basis. You may think it's a slightly unsavoury thing to do but I can assure you it isn't – and you will need to get your head around its place in a business, and home, environment.

If you find persuasion difficult and aren't really sure where to start in a business context, then the first thing you have to think about is creating a need. We will look at how you can achieve this in more detail later on in this book. You may also want to think about creating a brand that people simply have to have to feel as though they 'belong'. Many large, well-known designer brands do this very successfully.

For more information on how to persuade potential clients to use your business, check out this great article:

www.inspirationpro.net/9-powerful-techniques-for-persuading-people.

Listens to their gut feeling (intuition)

We all have those gut feelings that nag away at us every so often crying 'Listen to me, listen to me!', but how many of us actually do listen to them? Whenever I start work with a new group of budding entrepreneurs, I always ask that question. Lots of hands shoot up. When I ask who actually acts on their intuition, the hands start to waver. And therein lies a problem. We might listen but we don't act. In business, as in life, that's not always a good thing. And particularly when we are talking about gut feelings. I think that part of the problem is that we are taught to look at challenges and situations logically. And logic often defies itself. Sometimes we need to use our emotions, our creative side, to make a decision. We can't always be rational but we are taught to be so; told that if we can't work out the solution in an academic way, then that can't be the solution.

I have lost count of the number of times when, over the years, I've known the right course of action in my heart but my head has taken over and insisted that I follow it. And I've been wrong. Eventually I learnt – it took a long, long time in some instances – but learn I did, and now I always follow my instincts. I can't think of a single time when I've been proven wrong.

If you think about it logically, when you're setting up a business it becomes your baby. You spend so much time nurturing, growing and developing it that you become the expert not only on your business baby, but also on the industry in which it operates. There is little or nothing that you don't know – and your job is to carry on knowing more and more. After all, knowledge is power. Therefore, it is also logical that if a challenge or a scenario crops up in your business, you are the person most likely to know how to deal with it. You are the expert. And because you are the expert, in your heart you will know what to do. But there's our dilemma again. In your heart. That means relying on our intuition...

I say try it! Go with your gut instinct. Throw caution – and logic – to the wind and just let your heart tell you the answer. The first time is always the most difficult, as in most things, but when you've done it once it becomes easier and easier. Decision-making isn't always about using your head. It's also sometimes about using your heart. And when it's a business decision – and it's your business

– emotion, whatever we like to say about there being no emotion in business, really does have a part to play. Here, in any case.

Copes with uncertainty and complexity

One of the most uncertain games you can get into is that of running your own business, for the only certainty is the uncertainty. I will say that before we go any further. If you are looking for something nice and steady, 9 to 5, with four weeks' paid holiday and a Christmas party every year, then this isn't it. If you are the kind of person who wants something that is predictable and certain then, laudable a sentiment as that is, and as a single mum totally understandable, running your own business is not for you.

If, however, you are looking for a job where nothing is guaranteed; where your diary will say one thing but once the doors open for business it may well end up saying something else; where you will be desperately scrimping and saving for money one minute and then frantically invoicing as though it's gone out of fashion the next; and where you will meet the most extraordinary people and go to the most fascinating of places – then this is definitely your stop.

The very best thing for me about running my own businesses is the unpredictability. There are many things I love about being my own boss, and I've mentioned them before, but this is the real kick for me. I have never found a job that beats it. Ever. And I've had a few really great, enviable jobs in my time!

I think when you have a mind that never stays still, as I do, this is definitely a career consideration. I am an ideas person; constantly thinking, turning things over, finding solutions to problems, and so being able to exercise that brain through my work is a joy. There are very few jobs where you can do that.

However, I do understand that as a single mum unpredictability is not really what you need. There is enough uncertainty in your world without adding to it. But you can uncertainty-proof your business life to a degree. It's not as if you have absolutely no idea what will happen, it's just that you have to be prepared for anything to happen.

For instance, financially, you need to plan ahead. The one area of my life in which

I definitely don't embrace uncertainty is money. I've got used to it but that doesn't mean that I like it. So I put measures in place to try and negate any repercussions.

I have my financial forecasts for the next three months on a whiteboard. I continually update them so that I know, at a glance, where I am. If things are looking a bit dicey for one of the months, then I know I need to go all out to improve things. I always try to ensure that I have a basic month's salary in the business account so that if money doesn't come in on time (and that's not an unusual scenario), I can still pay the rent and feed my son.

Of course, the first twelve months of running a start-up is a bit trickier. You might as well stick your finger in the wind as forecast sales correctly, so you need to have something cleverer up your sleeve. I have lurched, if I am honest, from month to month in the first year of running all of my businesses. I have never started one with lots of money in the bank; I've always had little or nothing in the way of financial resources. I would imagine that there are few single mums who have. However, I have sold my shoe collection more times than I care to count, and have even resorted to selling my car, furniture, and clothes when pushed. But I'm still here. I'm still going. No one has suffered (although I really miss one pair of sparkly, strappy silver sandals even now) and I've always managed to keep the roof over our heads. So it was all good in the end. As it often is.

Builds trust with others

If you are going to grow a business on the back of first class suppliers, fabulous staff and loyal customers – you need to be able to build trusting relationships with other people. Some find that easy, some don't. However, it's also a life skill so if you discover that people find it difficult to trust you, you need to look at why. The most likely cause is the message you are giving out. Whether that's you personally, or your company. So how can you change that?

If you suspect it might be you, then look at how you speak to people. Are you friendly or a little brusque? Are you instantly friendly, or do you take a while to warm up to people? Is your body language very closed and defensive, or are you open and welcoming? Do you smile with your eyes and your voice, as well as your mouth? That might sound a bit odd but, believe me, the eyes give everything away.

You can also tell in an instant if someone isn't smiling down the phone when you speak to them. These are both very off-putting as well as guaranteed to put a potential client or member of your team on their guard.

If you suspect it might be your marketing, then think about what aspect it could be. Are you promising something that you obviously can't deliver? Is the message sanctimonious and patronising? Are the colours wrong, and the images out of place? (Both of these will have a direct impact on your marketing potential.) Do you really understand your potential clients? What are you like on the phone? Are you telling people that you offer a quick and easy service yet take an age to answer the phone, or don't return calls? All of these are obvious but when you are deep in the thick of planning and running a new business, they can sometimes slip through the net.

Whatever it is, act on it now.

Resilient

Life throws an awful lot of curved balls at us sometimes, and not always when we are best able to cope with them. So it's up to us to ride with the knocks as best we can. How we deal with challenges and difficult situations often marks us out as the person we truly are. Single mums have to be more resilient than most and that's why, potentially, they make such fantastic entrepreneurs and business owners. Being able to keep coming back from the challenges is a real plus.

I don't think we can really say that we aren't resilient; after all, as a friend of mine says, you survived being born, you survived the first year of life and here you are years later still surviving. We learn to be resilient as we go – nothing comes easy; most things are a test in one form or another and we get through one and move on to the next, sometimes in the blink of an eye.

Running a business takes a lot of resilience for, by its very nature, it's a world where knocks are to be expected. Remember, unless you are working as a freelancer on long term contracts, or buying a franchise, you are venturing into the unknown. There are no rules, no guarantees, no clear picture of how things may go. Apart, of course, from the fact that it's likely to be a rocky road for quite some time. Knocks can come in the form of financial setbacks, marketing failures, supplier or manufacturing issues, or just good, honest, general business mistakes. We all make them. As you encounter more challenges and then overcome them, your resilience grows stronger. You get better at dodging the problems and dealing with issues – and even arrive at a point where you can sometimes head off a crisis altogether. It just takes practice.

Literate and numerate

Although literate and numerate are listed separately on the table, I have put them together here, for I believe they not only highlight the same issues but are so closely linked that it seems sensible to discuss them both at the same time.

In business, as in life, it's extremely useful to have basic levels of literacy and numeracy. Being able to string a coherent sentence together – verbally and in writing – is such a plus, as well as being able to do basic sums – addition, subtraction, percentages. Most of us, if we haven't managed to grasp these skills particularly well in school, get a bit better at them outside in the big wide world once we see why they are useful and where they are used. When they are seen in context.

However, there is an assumption that you have to be brilliant at maths and English, particularly maths, to run a business. Not true. Some of the most entrepreneurial people I come across are those who struggle with either or both subjects, and some of our best loved entrepreneurs are dyslexic or dyspraxic themselves. When you see the world differently and deal with challenges in a different way because that's how your brain is wired, it means you learn many extra skills that go towards being able to then run a business too. Creative thinking, resilience, determination...

What you do need to be able to do, however, is to negate the effect those struggles may have on the day to day running of your business. It is one thing to find something tricky but another to let it, potentially, cause damage to your business when you could do something about it. So what could you do?

For those who find literacy difficult, there are spellchecker software packages available. Given how technology has developed over the last few years, there really is little excuse for sending out a poorly spelt email to a client. Imagine how you would feel if one was sent to you? Would you want to use that company? The chances are that you wouldn't.

If you find writing generally is troublesome for you, then there are a number of options. Perhaps you could ask a friend or family member to compose a set of generic emails and marketing pieces for you, whilst you dictate what you want them to say? You can then send them out when appropriate. Or you could hire a specialist. Of course, there is an inherent cost to that but investing in your weaknesses is always a good business move. Eventually you will be in a position to hire someone to work in your company on a permanent basis, and they can then be responsible for the areas that you find tricky.

If maths is your weakness then join the club! Nice to meet you – it's mine too! The number of hands that shoot up whenever I ask a new group who finds this topic difficult is shocking. Yet they also think you need to be really good at maths to run a business. I am proof this isn't the case. You need to be able to master the basics but you don't need to be a mathematical genius.

I am dyscalculic which, to simplify things, is the numbers version of dyslexia. I can do basic sums, I'm actually really good at mental arithmetic, and I'm quite good at percentages of figures (although I have never been able to figure out greater than percentages). Anything more complicated? I'm done for. I used to cry in maths lessons. It was as though the teacher was speaking a foreign language. In fact they may as well have been, for what they said meant nothing to me. There was nothing for me to hook what was said onto.

My parents didn't believe me when I said that I found maths hard. They just thought I was being lazy. You may have had that experience too, which knocks your confidence in the subject, and your abilities, further. Don't let it carry on knocking your confidence. To be able to deal with these two areas, which are really important, you will have to grit your teeth, forget the past and move on to the future – having put structures in place to help.

So, if you find maths tough what can you do? First thing I recommend is to find a really good bookkeeper and/or accountant. Explain to them that you struggle to understand basic concepts and ask for their help. My accountant is fabulous and I know that if I have any problems I can pick up the phone and ask. Of course, there is a cost involved in taking professional advice (they are running a business too after all) but it's money well spent. I'm extremely lucky that my eldest son does my books for me so, again, I can ask him to explain figures and work out the trickier calculations for me.

When it comes to sitting in front of a client and discussing prices, you will need to be on top of your game more so than other business owners perhaps, because you find this stuff difficult. My recommendation is to already have some costs and prices in front of you. If you are thinking of offering a discount then, again, have those figures in front of you – ready calculated. Anything more complicated can be answered with, 'Let me go away and put some figures together for you. I can have them with you by the end of the day/tomorrow morning.' It might sound like a cop out but it's actually the sensible way to go. Don't do what I've done before and make a complete mess of financial negotiations, then walk away not only out of pocket but looking like an idiot because the client knows you had no idea what you were talking about. Be prepared!

In practice, as long as you know what's going in and out of the company accounts each month, and can do basic maths, you're going to be OK. Just plug the knowledge gap.

Risk taker

Everything we do involves an element of risk. From getting out of bed, to boiling the kettle, to crossing the road – even sharing the air with others. At some point, we are going to face the results of our risk. Of course, the majority of things that we do carry little risk and the result of that risk is quite minimal. We all have levels of risk that we are comfortable with, and levels that we are not – and therein lies the answer to the oft asked question: 'Ali, didn't you worry about the risk you took as a single mum in setting up your own business?'

Answer? No.

I'm a bit of a risk junkie in my professional life. I love taking risks – seeing what I can challenge myself to do next, what I can achieve. I love taking nothing and making something – and that involves risk.

Now, on a personal level, I'm the absolute opposite. I don't like risk at all; which might surprise you, as running a business has an impact on both parts of your life. However, I put some risk-proofing in place in terms of my finances, which were my big worry (not being able to feed and clothe my son, and keep a roof over our heads was the 3am panic), and so far so good. I won't deny that there have been some slightly scary moments, but all in all, the risk has been worth it and I've loved every second of the journey so far.

It's an accepted fact that running a business is pretty risky. There are no two ways about it. You stake what money you may have on the slim chance that a plan you've spent some time working on will pay off. That your vocational or professional expertise will prove to be more popular than someone else's, and that you will be able to use it, along with your personal skills, to make money.

Now, I'm simplifying things massively here – and I will show you throughout this book how I absolutely believe you can do all of the above – but the point is still the same. If you want to get on in life – learn, love, succeed – then you need to take a risk. Decide on the level you are happy with (don't exceed it when you start your business until there is evidence that it, and you, can take it) and then bit by bit you learn more, you challenge yourself more, you risk more, and you grow more. It's a lovely circle.

Why didn't I worry about taking a risk to set up my first business as a single mum? Oddly enough it was the least risky of the two scenarios on offer at the time – work or self-employment – and I knew it would pay off. I thought about it, I weighed up the pros and cons, and the odds, and decided it was the better thing for my family and for me at the time. And I was right.

Why then, five years on, having started a brand new career as a lecturer, did I do it all again? That, surely, was even riskier? Maybe. But for me, being happy was worth it.

You don't need to be a massive risk taker to run a business, you just need to be aware that the risk is there. If you are the kind of person who would never take a risk ever, the mere idea of it bringing you out in a cold sweat, then you might want to think carefully about setting up on your own. That's not to say that you couldn't do it – of course you could. I refer you back to my point about the level of risk. It's just that it's a risky thing to do in general. Still not for you? You might want to use up your Risk Points on something a bit less hazardous instead.

Talents

We've discussed skills, which are so very important, but now we need to look at our talents. Now, I can guarantee that there will be some amongst you who are reading this, shaking your heads and saying, 'I don't have any talents. I'm not good at anything.'

Wrong! And tsk at you for doubting yourself.

We are all good at something; it's just a question of finding out what it is. It might be looking after animals or kids; it might be icing cakes; it might be chatting; it might be cleaning. Whatever it is, and however random it might seem, there is a business idea in everything somewhere. You just need to look carefully, put on your Creative Thinking Hat, and the idea will start to form.

For those of you who have no idea what kind of business you might want to run and would like some ideas, have a look at the Skills Audit below. It's a useful way of drawing out your innate potential and identifying what you could build on for your business.

When you complete this, think of as many things as possible that you like to do and that you believe you're good at. Don't feel constrained by the lines – if you have twenty-five personal skills then find another piece of paper and write them all down.

Practical skills e.g. writing, DIY, cooking

Personal skills e.g. listening, caring

Things you like to do outside of work/the home e.g. hobbies

What environment do you like to work in?

What job would you like to do?

How would your friends describe you?

You might be surprised by the last question: 'How would your friends describe you?' You might wonder what this has to do with your business idea. Actually, it has a lot to do with it. Often, we don't see what's in front of our noses. We think we portray one thing when, in fact, we may portray another. It's our friends who see that. Think of what they have said to you in the past about you – nice things I'm sure! What have they said that you're good at? What have they said are your strengths? Have they ever said what job they think you'd be suited to? Write it all down.

Now, what does this exercise tell you about yourself? Read your answers as a whole answer, not as individual responses. Mix and match them. Put some of the skills with the environment you like to work in. Some of the things you like to do outside of work/the home with what people say about you. Is there something that jumps out at you that you might never have thought of before? Perhaps you've always wanted to work outside and your friends tell you that you are an independent person. And you love DIY. I can see a potential business there. Maybe you love kids, want to work at home, and are very artistic. I can see a potential business there too.

We're not looking for the next big corporate here – we're looking for a business that you could set up and run alongside your other commitments; that fulfils and rewards you. Not every business has to be the next Virgin.

If necessary, keep adding to this over the next few days. Don't feel pressured into having to do it right now. Planning a business isn't something that can be done in an hour or two with a coffee – it takes an awful lot of time and effort and, as I've already said, the 'You' part of it is as important as the idea. Take as long as you need.

So, we've looked at the skills a business owner needs, and we've discussed them in some detail and, hopefully, you have been able to identify your individual areas of strength and areas for improvement.

We've also looked at talents – which we all have, whatever we might think – via a Skills Audit, and your mind will now be buzzing with the things you think you might be interested in developing into a business. Great!

Now you need to take those areas for improvement and find a way of making them better or delegating to someone who can do them on your behalf. Don't think that just because you've been through the motions, that's enough. It isn't. Being an entrepreneur is all about being a person of action. So if that's who you want to be, you need to demonstrate that to yourself and others around you by attending courses – online or otherwise – and securing the services of friends or professionals who can help you. It's only by doing this that you can start to build on what you have, and to develop your business idea – and yourself – into a thriving organisation.

And having completed your Skills Audit you've got a great idea, or perhaps a couple, that you'd like to explore via a business plan to see what potential they may have.

So what are we waiting for? Let's get cracking.

CASE STUDY

Raquel Masco

From an early age Raquel wanted to run her own business. Now 41 and single mum to a 17-year-old son, Raquel runs Rocky's Concierge Service, which includes event design/planning, cleaning/organising and errand running. Raquel is also co-founder of a non-profit organisation for single mothers, SingleMoms Created4Change. She is based in Texas, USA.

I have always wanted to own my own business. Even though I was employed I wanted to bring in extra income to my household and do what I enjoyed doing. Running my own business full time was the beginning of me discovering who I was and who I could be. It was overwhelming, intimidating and exhilarating all at the same time. I had to face a rough economy, scepticism, and my own insecurities. I had to face evictions, and bills paid but not enough to buy food. Every time I came to a place where I was ready to give up I regrouped and started over. I've learned patience, perseverance and that everything that happens is a learning experience. The first wedding I did was wonderful. It was for over 200 guests and we not only pulled it off, we made some real memories. Pleasing my clients is success, as is coming home to my family. I founded SingleMomsCreated4Change after years of seeing others go through hard times as well as my own challenges as a single mother. Our mission is to assist and empower single moms to live above and beyond even their own expectations. We are an outreach organisation that in turn gives our moms opportunities to reach out into their community. I hope the future will bring growth of the business and positive change. We've had some great highs and low-lows, and I amgrateful for it all.

Website: www.singlemoms-created4change.com

Chapter 5: **Your business – Pre Start-up**

Before you start up your business, or even start writing a business plan, there are some things you will need to think about.

- Timing

- Equipment/resources needed

- Balancing a business and family

Timing

There are a number of practicalities that you need to consider before starting a business, particularly when you are a single mum, and probably the most important of these is timing. Is this the right time for you, and your family, to start up on your own?

I guess the retort could be, 'Is there ever a right time for anything?' and, yes, I understand that sentiment, but it comes from a negative mindset and we are all about being positive.

You must consider whether you will have the time to devote to the planning, even before looking at the time you will need to put into running a business. Is this commitment compatible with where your family is right now? Do you have a lot of other obligations that are, perhaps, of more importance at this point in your life? Are you yourself lacking in the motivation to do something like this? Do you think that a bit of time working on yourself and your emotions – how you see yourself – would be a good start before tackling the Start-Up Beast? That's no bad thing! Congratulations for realising it if so! Many women take up some kind of coaching programme that focuses on these sorts of things before they either start back in work or start up a business. It not only helps with self-esteem and confidence but also gets you into the mindset of research and learning if you haven't been in that zone for some time.

Looking in depth at where you all are, not just where you are, is a very positive thing to do. Too many people – of all ages and backgrounds – think that setting up a business is just a question of researching and writing a business plan. Not until some time down the line do they realise that, of equal importance, is considering what's going on at a personal level too, because it has such an impact on their ability to make a success of their project. Feeling fuzzy headed and lacking direction will merely translate into your business.

Take some time to consider, very honestly, whether this really is the right time for you. And, if not, when would be? And plan towards that instead. We all know how quickly time flies when we're doing something productive. Before you know it, you'll be writing that business plan and working towards your bright new future.

Equipment/resources needed

As part of your business plan, we will be looking in detail at start-up costs and the equipment that you will need to run your business. However, I am a great believer in being prepared, so now is the time to start thinking about what you might need and, crucially, what you already have so that you can at least have the basics up and ready.

Space

Where will you work from? If at home, do you have a corner that you can pin your colours to and deem yours? Is it easily child-proofed if needs be? If not, how will you deal with that? If not at home, is it easily accessible from the other places you need to go to – school, childminder, nursery?

Equipment

You'll need a desk or some form of workspace. But it doesn't have to be a desk in the traditional sense of the word. It could be a kitchen table (lots of women set up businesses using their kitchen table for all manner of things, including production space). It could be a dressing table. It could be an old door set on two sturdy tea-chests. It doesn't matter what it looks like, it just needs to be serviceable.

You'll need a phone. I've noticed that lots of people don't use landlines any more, they rely on mobiles. Once upon a time this was frowned on in business, and there was an element of clients not being sure it was a bona fide business if it was operated from a mobile. Nowadays, however, taking into account our frenetic lifestyles, mobiles are the way to go. But just because you have a personal phone number, don't think you can use that for business too. That's a no-no.

First, let's say you are lucky enough to be whisked away on an evening out and you have a great time. Next morning, having left your phone on, it rings at 8am. You pick it up, murmuring a groggy hello into the handset, feeling as though your mouth doesn't belong to you. And it's a client. I'll say no more.

Secondly, you need to switch off. Running a business is stressful. Running a family and household singlehandedly is stressful. The two together?! Clients don't always respect business working hours. After all, if they are working then they will sometimes assume you are too. Or they just might want to leave a phone message rather than send an email. If your phone is on, you're going to get the call. I've had calls at 11pm before. On a Saturday night. It's not family friendly.

So – you need a separate number. We've all got an old handset knocking around somewhere that can be utilised, and you can use a PAYG sim card. Put a friendly answerphone message on, giving your name, the company name, and the assurance that you will call back as soon as possible. Job done. Then turn it on five minutes before you start work to collect messages, and turn it off when the office closes. No excuses.

You're going to need a computer and an internet connection. Most of us have these now but I appreciate that not everyone does, and they're a necessity. If you don't have a computer, there are schemes available to help you get one. If you are currently claiming benefits, it's worth talking to your local benefits office to check out whether they can help. If not (and I understand you might feel a bit nervous doing this), try calling a large local company to see if they are getting rid of any old computers. Companies often update these sorts of items and they get taken to landfill. Better to go to a local start-up business surely?

If not, try eBay (although be careful – people have been caught out buying this sort of thing on auction sites), or local second-hand retailers. Forget the idea of having to have everything new. When you start up a business, second- or even third-hand becomes your best friend.

Alternatively, do a bit of research at the library, using their computers, and see if your local council has any start-up schemes. My local council has recently been funding laptops and phones for those wanting to start their own business, for instance.

Printer, paper, pens etc

You'll also need the usual assorted miscellaneous items to get started. No need for anything flashy, it just needs to be serviceable. As you run your business, believe me, you'll end up collecting pens, paperclips and other stationery items to the degree that you feel you could open your own shop. Pound shops are a great place for these sorts of things. AND REMEMBER TO KEEP THE RECEIPTS FOR ANYTHING YOU BUY – no matter how small or seemingly insignificant! We'll be talking more about these later in the book.

Balancing a business and family

Planning and then starting up a business is a time-intensive exercise. It soon becomes an all-consuming passion, with more and more of your energy poured in to develop the potential that you have uncovered.

Running a family and a household singlehandedly is also very time-intensive. Add in setting up a business and then starting to run it, and you can see how easily overbalanced life can become. So what can you do to try to ensure that this doesn't happen to you?

First, be aware that it may happen! Forewarned is forearmed and if you know that this may be a possibility, you can look out for the warning signs so that you can head off any possible problems.

The second thing you can do is to look at your day as a whole. How can you spread everything you need to do across it so that no one loses? Most single mum with businesses work around their kids' social and sleeping patterns. So, for instance in the business planning stage, if your child always goes to a particular afterschool club, use that time to do some more work on your business plan. Other solutions that mums have found are to get up a bit earlier or work once the kids are in bed. Not rocket science of course but proof that this kind of time management works.

If you are lucky enough to have a great support network, perhaps someone would have your kids, or mind them for you at your home, whilst you spend an hour or two on your plan or seeing banks and potential clients.

When it comes to running the business itself, one of the easiest solutions is to consider whether this needs to be a full-time venture to start with if your children are still young, and possibly pre-nursery/school. There are women who run businesses with babies, and they don't rely on nannies or hired help, but they do have to be extraordinarily disciplined when it comes to time management and prioritising tasks. This works really well for an online business, for instance – it doesn't matter when you work, your business is always open 24/7. For those offering a service, it may be more difficult to balance meeting clients and caring for very young children, so it makes sense to schedule appointments between certain hours so that everyone knows when is working time, and when is home time.

It is important to schedule home time. Don't get so consumed by your business that you forget about making time for your family too. There will be many readers shaking their heads at this statement, thinking that they would never do that. Believe me, those of us who have started businesses as single mums will all confirm that we thought that at first too – but did it anyway. It's an easy trap to fall into, so make sure that you are very strict with yourself regarding the hours that you work. If there is something really important that simply can't be avoided – and that does happen – then either try to do it when your children are otherwise engaged, or do it, and then spend a bit of extra time with them afterwards to compensate.

Of course, as your children get older it is easier to schedule in some work time when they become more independent and don't want Mum around so much – I'm in that stage right now. They do still need to have some time with you, however, so don't get completely carried away with the new flexibility you have and become too absorbed in your business. It can grow to be such a passion that running the risk of turning into a workaholic is greater than you may think!

Keep some time for you, and for your kids – work isn't everything.

So, a balance between home and business can be achieved. There are lots of single mum business owners to bear testament to the fact, but it does involve great commitment, energy and organisation. Having said that, given that single mums are already used to having to employ these skills in large quantities, it shouldn't be too difficult to schedule in a bit of business planning too...

So – you have thought through the practicalities and got them covered off. Now we need to tackle your idea.

I find that those I work with fall into two camps – those with one firm idea, and those with lots of potential ideas. Neither of these are bad scenarios. It's great that some people come along with a very definite idea of what they want to do for their business but, as an entrepreneur, it's also a pre-requisite that you are an ideas person, so lots of ideas is a good place to work from too.

I always have plenty of ideas on the go. I have what I call a 'spider-brain' – one that continually sees links and hook-ups – so I can't focus on my businesses for long without seeing something else that might be complementary to the services we already offer, or even a brand new idea altogether. It's hard when you have that kind of mind because you have to be even more focused than usual in order to get things done. Of course, from a business point of view it's an asset. However, the trick is to realise which of the many ideas is the best one to start with.

If you are someone with lots of ideas then I'm fairly sure you will have a favourite. Even though you may not realise it, there's one that you're likely to be most keen on. Unfortunately, it may not always be the right one to kick off your career as an entrepreneur. The one you are looking for is the one that will make you the most money with the least amount of investment, or associated problems. That's the one that will enable you to start considering some of your other ides and, potentially, to indulge your favourite idea in the future.

The best way to assess which is Idea One is to be ruthless. Look at each idea with no emotion, through someone else's eyes, and weigh it up against the others. Just like cream in milk, there will naturally be a couple that rise to the surface. They are the ones that you want to research further.

You then need to write a business plan for them. I wouldn't recommend doing this for more than a couple of ideas, three at the most, given the time it takes, so you need to be very ruthless at the earlier stage. Keep going back and assessing until you are left with only three ideas. That will then give you a much better view of the situation and help you to decide which is the idea you can go forward with.

Don't think that you have to write off the others, far from it. I have notes full of ideas dating back years, and also a couple of businesses in my heart for the future, but I'm just not in the right place to work with them quite yet. But that's OK. I will be one day. Just as you will too!

CASE STUDY

Conor, 16, is at school.

The first time I became aware that my mum was an entrepreneur was in 2006, when I was 7 years old. She had set up her own media company and had sat me down and explained that she was now going to work for herself. I decided that I wanted to help, so I made an open/closed sign for her office door. I have seen mum battle her way through all the hardships that both her personal life and business has thrown at her, and she has got through it all. She is a role model to me and is inspirational. I've learnt that true success doesn't occur overnight, and that you shouldn't just give up when life gets difficult, that instead you should just keep trying. In the future I would like a stable job, which pays well and helps to keep my finances balanced. I believe my mum has helped me to want this. I want to be able to wake up in the morning knowing that I have impacted people's lives positively.

Chapter 6: Your business – Business Planning

'Get up and at it!' Ali Golds

So, you're still thinking of starting your own business? I haven't put you off yet? Great news!

So, business plans. Everyone knows that it's the recommended thinking to write one when you are looking at starting a business. I can't think of one scenario where it wouldn't be recommended and certainly the big name entrepreneurs urge the same. However, a business plan is slightly more than a tick box exercise. Number one on the 'I Want To Start A Business So What Do I Do First?' list. It's a living document. It's there to be regularly reviewed and updated so that you have something to work towards and with during those first few uncertain months and as you start to grow your business.

Mind you, I was guilty of doing exactly the same myself. When I set up my first business with my ex-husband, I had read the books that said write a business plan too. So I did. And when I'd finished it, I put it on the shelf in our office and never read it or referred to it again. Kind of defeated the object of the exercise.

A couple of years on, I was asked by our bank manager if he could see the business plan. I took him over a copy of the original – beautifully presented. He looked at it. He looked at me. He put it down on the desk, folded his hands and said, 'This year's, Ali?' I think the look on my face was answer enough.

Now, I'm also going to be honest and say that writing a business plan can be extraordinarily tedious. It can seem like a mountain too high to climb for those of us who don't much like paperwork and just want to crack on with the idea and see how it goes. Much as I would like to say that I agree with you, I'm not much of a fan of spending hours on a few sheets of paper myself, on balance I'm afraid that I can't. A business plan really is incredibly useful. Vital. It shows you where the gaps in your business are, where the issues will arise, and how you can adjust or modify your idea for a greater chance of success. Even whether it's worth it at all. Surely a bit of fingernail-gnawing and hair-pulling is worth knowing that?

Now some people will tell you that you don't need a business plan at all and others will say that you can write one on one side of A4. As we all know, some people will say anything to get out of doing a thing properly, so I wouldn't take much notice of these sorts of comments. The people that matter – i.e. investors, bank managers, suppliers, you – will require sight of a business plan at some point. No business plan equals no plan of action. I understand the thinking behind that – stifling creativity etc – but it's not a good enough reason not to write one. And one side of A4 isn't going to cover a business plan adequately enough for a start-up. Particularly for someone who has never run a business before. I'm not saying that it needs to be War and Peace. It doesn't. But it does need to cover all of the salient points, and to allow you to explore and investigate the potential of your business. One page just won't cut it.

As you go through the book you will see that I have written the sections based around a business plan. A pro-forma version is also downloadable from my website

www.aligolds.com

There are many variations on a theme when it comes to business plans – you will know that if you've ever taken your life in your hands and googled the topic. It's overwhelming and enough to put someone off even looking for one! However, they all need to contain the same sorts of information and cover the same points – so as long as yours does, you're OK. I will be detailing the sections that need covering as we go, so you won't run the risk of missing something out that's important.

Also, please remember that this is YOUR business plan. So whilst the pro-forma is generic, you can tinker with it to make it applicable to your business and your business only. If something doesn't apply to you, then don't include it. If something needs more explanation than the box allows, then expand on it. Don't feel constrained.

OK. So the point of a business plan is to answer the 'what ifs?' It's an exercise in scenario planning and, given that you may well have little or no information to go on in certain sections, you have to research as much as you can to try to negate the chance of any nasty surprises. To a degree, it's also a finger in the wind exercise. There'll be some guesstimating going on, albeit educated guesstimating, but guesstimating nonetheless. That's why it's a living document; as you go, you will be able to update figures (usually the part where most of the guesstimating happens) and start to build a better and more reliable picture of where your business is going.

When I wrote my very first business plan, I didn't have a clue about the figures. We've already identified my issues around numbers so you can see that this was likely to be my weakness. At that point, I hadn't taken my good advice about asking someone for help either (totally convinced I could do it on my own – I didn't need help!). So I had written it myself. It was pretty good and rather impressive – even if I say so myself – until we got to the numbers. I had forecast a first year turnover of £100k. From a standing start. Pretty remarkable! Or pretty wrong! Depending upon your point of view...

The bank manager nearly fell over when he read it, and was convinced by my long and detailed explanations (it was my passion, don't forget – and when something is your passion you believe in it 100 per cent and some; and everyone you speak to will come away believing exactly the same). His eyes were shining, and he offered us the earth. Thank goodness we didn't take it – my predictions were out by 35k. We didn't make a loss, we made a nice profit in any case, but it does go to prove the point. You may think you know but in reality, when it comes to planning a start-up, you rarely do.

Writing a business plan gives you the chance to go back to the drawing board as many times as you need to before you take the leap into the unknown. The step off the cliff in the dark. But with a good plan, you'll have a map and a torch to aid your journey.

SECTION ONE: EXECUTIVE SUMMARY

The first thing you will see once you look at the plan is the Executive Summary. This is, in essence, the one side of A4 business plan that I spoke of earlier, but it sits within the entire document, and it is completed once you've completed the plan. So we aren't going to worry about it right now – we'll come back to it later.

SECTION TWO: BUSINESS DETAILS

When I deliver my start-up programme, this is probably my favourite bit to talk about. That might seem a little strange (surely there are much more interesting things in a business plan?), but actually this is the place where you can save a lot of heartache and stave off some big problems if you get it right first time. It's more complicated than it might at first seem.

Company name

I don't know about you but I find coming up with a company name the hardest part of setting up a business. I agonise for what seems like forever, with either no inspiration at all or inspiration that appears to have come from another planet and bears no resemblance to the company I'm trying to form.

And it's such an important thing to get right. It's like a personal name; your company is going to go through its life with this moniker – no changing halfway through once you've spent a fortune on marketing and brand recognition activities. I know that there are companies that have changed and adapted their names – confectionery companies seem keen on changing brand names every so often, for instance – but it doesn't always pay off, and I wouldn't recommend it unless it's an extreme circumstance. Your business is going to be judged on its name and people will come to their own conclusions about what it stands for – just on the basis of a handful of letters. It needs to appeal to the target market, as well as not put off any other potential clients. It needs to be easily spelt and remembered.

When I set up my company Operation Enterprise, I chose the name because it signified action (operation) and also mentioned what the company was involved in (enterprise). After about six months, I realised that my clients (FE colleges) didn't really know what enterprise was. In fact, no one seemed to know what enterprise was – and those that did had completely differing opinions from one another. Also, when I mentioned the word in staff training sessions it yielded arguments from some teachers who didn't think that business should be a part of education. I fast realised that enterprise was a contentious word, so I was going to stop using it. But it was – is – half of my company name. You can see the dilemma.

This begs the question, how should you choose your company name? Should you put words in it that describe what you do or should you make it vague and mysterious? Should you use initials only (quite popular) or just one random word that may have nothing at all to do with your business area but is very evocative? As long as you can tie in your name with your business, and it's not offensive, then you are pretty free to do what you want.

However, a few things to think about:

- Using offensive words (even if you don't think they are) or phrases, or even something that has an offensive connotation, is a bad idea. If you want to set your business up as a limited company you won't be able to use such words in any case. And how many customers are you going to get if you have a controversial company name? Not many, I'd bet.

- Beware of giving your company a name that is similar to another company's. There are many instances of corporates taking legal action against little companies for trying to trade off their name. You may not be doing that, and it may be the furthest thing from your mind, but the management of the other company may well not agree. You'd do the same in their shoes – particularly if your company is a wholesome organisation, and the other company isn't. It's all about defending reputation and brand. Steer clear of being a copycat.

- Also bear in mind the potential problems of using the name of a company that is no longer trading. You have no idea why it failed – and could well see your company fail too as a result. You may also be in contempt of The Insolvency Act. Don't be tempted.

- Using your own name might seem like a good idea and, after all, lots of companies do it. Joe Bloggs and Daughters. Josephine Bloggs and Sons. Family firms are a fantastic high street institution, and there are many examples of them. However, be aware that this can potentially cause problems for you if your business fails. Consider using part of your name, rather than all of it – or a combination of initials – to be sure.

Address

Starting up a business is an expensive thing to do. Resist the temptation to hire an office or workshop space of your own straight away, and look for alternatives. Do you have a spare corner of a room at home that you can use? Can you share some space with a friend? Can you sub-let space from another company? Creative and artistic businesses often share a large workshop space, keeping down the costs for them all. Rarely does a start-up need a brand spanking new office, with all of the expense that this entails, and with the advent of online shopping and other such technological advances, many don't get one.

I have a lot of entrepreneurial friends who run their businesses from coffee houses and on the train in between meetings. If you need an official address, and don't want to use your home one, then your accountant will happily let you use his or her address for a fee. Alternatively, you can use a virtual office address. Some of the swankiest addresses are hired out to companies just like ours!

If you are choosing to work from home, please be aware of the following restrictions:

- If you are renting from a social housing organisation, the lease will state that you cannot run a business from home. This is usually to stop people running hair salons and the like from a residential area, but it's always advisable to check your own landlord's position on this before you start trading. The last thing you want is to find that you've broken the terms of your lease and get evicted.

- The same applies to private tenants. Please check with your landlord.

- You also need to speak to your local council regarding business rates for the portion of your property that you use to run your business from. The likelihood is that you will not be liable, particularly if just working from a desk in a communal area, e.g. a sitting room or dining room, but again, it is always advisable to check before you start trading.

If you are running a limited company (and we will get on to those shortly), your name and private address will be listed on the registration documents at Companies House. There are various things that can be done to lessen the impact of this, including using a service address for all correspondence (most people use their accountant) rather than your home address, but there are steps you can take to keep your address private if this is of importance. Check out the Companies House website for more information.

Telephone number

Nowadays, most people work from mobiles so landlines are becoming increasingly rare – particularly for those people, like me, who work as a consultant or trainer. We are out and about all the time, so a mobile is the best number to catch us on. However, there are drawbacks to them. I am the first to admit that it doesn't look quite as professional to have only a mobile number rather than a landline or office number. Maybe I'm from the old school of business but I trust someone with a landline. And, yes, I do see the irony in that statement, as I don't use a landline myself!

You can, of course, get around this by renting an 0845 or 0800 number or one of the many other versions. You can re-direct all calls to your mobile so that it looks as though you are sitting in an office and picking up the call – but beware, depending upon the prefix number you choose, you will pay for the re-direction. Of course, if you'd rather you didn't, you can choose one where your client will!

However you choose to operate your telephone requirements, you will need a dedicated business line. There is no room for half-baked arrangements here. As explained in chapter 5, using your personal number for business is a definite no-no.

Not only do you need to be prepared for work each day – the 'open for business' mindset – but your clients need to be as well. It doesn't take more than one or two instances of your mobile being left on into the evening, or your picking up the landline number, for clients to realise that you work all hours – and they will ring you. At first, you might not think this is a bad thing. You want the work, and you'll go the extra mile to get it. I understand that. I've been there, I've done it. However, believe me, eventually it takes its toll and you will become resentful. You need a break. You need to draw lines between work and home, particularly as a single mum, or your kids will become resentful too as they see their time with their mum eroded away by her work. That's not what you want, and not healthy.

So, find an old phone and buy a PAYG sim card. Top up enough for the calls you think you'll make (you'll get used to budgeting for this after a few months), put a friendly greeting on the answer phone, and you're set. Please make sure that you do leave a personalised message by the way; there's nothing worse than ringing a business number only to find that you get the generic message. Firstly, it doesn't confirm that you've rung the correct number and secondly, what does it say about the business owner? Couldn't be bothered to even record a message. Not in the least professional.

Then decide on the times you will have your phone on, and stick to them.

Legal status

There are three main legal statuses that you will need to consider for your business. I always recommend that anyone setting up a new company takes advice on which one suits them best – an accountant will help here – but listed below are the options and some information on each to help you understand them, and the implications.

Before we carry on, you will need to fully understand the concept of liability. In business, as in life generally, liability means something that you are responsible for. At home this could be anything – children, housing, pets; in a business, we tend to talk about liability in relation to monies owed.

There are two types of liability; unlimited and limited. Unlimited liability means that your personal responsibility (liability) for the money is unlimited – in essence, whatever the debt is, and however much it may amount to, you owe it personally.

Limited liability, on the other hand, means that you have a limited personal responsibility (liability), and the company itself shoulders the majority of the responsibility (liability) for the debt.

In some businesses there is no debt as they have no suppliers, and take little or no monies up front from customers, so they operate on a very simple financial basis. Most businesses, however, have some level of debt and therefore liability starts to become more of an issue.

Sole trader

A sole trader is one person who owns and runs a business. There is no legal distinction between the two. The sole trader owns all of the business assets, operates under the position of unlimited liability and is, therefore, liable for any business debts. All of the profits belong to the sole trader.

Setting up initially as a sole trader is a popular route for those people starting a business on their own. There is little in the way of paperwork compared to the other statuses and this appeals to those who are dipping their toes in the water of self-employment.

A good example of a sole trader is a window cleaner. They have no suppliers – needing only buckets, shampoo, cloths and chamois leathers (all paid for as the window cleaner goes), plus ladders, a tank to hold the water and a van of some kind. If the sole trader is canny, she will have invested a little money in the more expensive resources plus some initial marketing up front, and purchased an older van rather than taking on the burden of a loan or lease on a new one. Therefore, she has no business debt. She also collects money for her window cleaning services as she goes, rarely being paid in advance.

Now, let's say that our window cleaner – out in all weathers – has an accident when climbing the ladder and can't work. The accident is actually quite serious, and she is now out of action for eight weeks. Who will bring income into her home? How will she pay her bills? How will she carry on running her business and servicing any debts it owes?

Well, there's nothing we can do about the first two worries, but the third? If she has no debt, then she has no problem. Yes, she obviously requires an income but from the point of view of unlimited liability, she owes nothing related to her business so is responsible for nothing.

However, let's say that she didn't take my sage advice and had taken out a loan for her van, had her accident, and now can't work. And she has to carry on with the repayments irrespective of this. Except she can't because she doesn't have any income and is relying on her savings, which won't stretch to paying her van loan as well as everything else. This is where being a sole trader can be potentially problematic, because if you are responsible for the debts and you can't pay, your creditor (the person to whom you owe money) can pursue you personally whether the debt is personal or business. Remember there is no distinction between you and your business. You are one and the same.

Ultimately, if you are unable to pay your debts, this can lead to bankruptcy. And bankruptcy, whilst it can be over within a year depending upon the level of your debts, stays on your credit record for six years – affecting a large part of your life.

I appreciate that what I have written may seem rather brutal. However, it's my job to outline worst case scenarios for you, and I wouldn't want you to go into something without being completely aware of what you are doing and the potential implications. Of course, you can avoid getting into this situation by trying not to run up debt – easier said than done, I appreciate – or having some money in reserve to cover any debt. And, assuming you've taken my advice and gone to speak to an accountant, they will talk you through all of this in any case, helping you to trade successfully and manage your business effectively, as a sole trader.

Other things to think about:

- It is your responsibility to notify HMRC when you go into business as a sole trader. If you don't tell them, they won't know. Don't put yourself in this position – it is very important that HMRC are aware of the change in your tax situation. Check out their website www.hmrc.gov.uk

  - Banks are less likely to lend to a sole trader.

- When you die, the business dies with you so, potentially, there could be no re-sale value. Considering all your hard work, that would be a shame.

Partnership

There are two types of partnership – limited and unlimited. These, of course, relate to the level of liability as previously discussed. Partnerships are often used in professional circles – doctors, lawyers, accountants, for example; however, anyone – assuming there is more than one of you of course – can set up in business as a partnership.

There are various requirements around registering your partnership, both legally and for taxation purposes, but one of the main things to sort out is a partnership agreement.

Anyone setting up a business with someone else, regardless of who they are, will need an agreement. It may be your best friend or your mum – it doesn't matter – you will need an agreement. Too many partnerships end in bitterness because one or more things haven't been done the way that everyone envisaged and, because there is nothing in writing, you can't show evidence of the way you thought things were to be run.

I am going to tell you a salutary tale.

When I set up my very first business, all those years ago, I was completely clueless about the legalities. I knew the business stuff, and was completely sure that I could build the company and its revenue – and my ex was a fantastically talented carpenter, but the legal side was an unknown.

We were recommended to a local accountant by our bank manager, and went to meet him one morning to talk about the business and, potentially, engage him as our company accountant. He was a very nice chap, a bit stern but extremely knowledgeable. We talked about our idea, he made some notes, and then he stopped writing and looked at us.

'So you'll need a partnership agreement.'

We looked at each other and laughed embarrassedly.

'Oh we don't need one of those,' I glibly said. 'We're married.'

'You might be,' he replied. 'But you should still have a partnership agreement.'

I think we agreed just to shut him up. And when we left, it was never mentioned again.

The years went past – five in fact. The business, at this point, was doing very well and we had a rather nice lifestyle. We'd sold our house the previous year to invest the money into the business, and planned to buy again during the following twelve months.

And then we split up. Rather acrimoniously, as you already know.

I was in a very vulnerable position; I'd lost so much of my life in a short space of time, so when my ex said I couldn't work in the business any more, I just agreed. In the space of three weeks I lost everything.

The moral of this story? If we'd had a partnership agreement, I'd have had something to back me up and support me – irrespective of my emotional state, and how I was feeling at the time, and what I thought I needed to agree with to keep everyone happy – and I would have been in a much better financial position. As it was, I couldn't afford a lawyer as my ex refused to pay me any maintenance for our son or give me what was owed to me from the business, so I got nothing. Twelve months later he had run the business into the ground, transferred the assets to another company that he ran with his friend, and that was the end of five years of extraordinarily hard work – and my dreams. I was left with nothing. No house, no car (he took that), no income, no job. It was an extremely difficult time and one that I wouldn't wish on anyone.

If you learn one thing from this story, please make it this: if you set up a business with someone else – GET A PARTNERSHIP AGREEMENT DRAWN UP! Don't leave it, and say you'll do it another day. Do it the minute you agree to work with someone. It's too easy to forget or put off, and is one of those things that you never know you need until you need it – and if you don't have it? Well, I've told you what happened to me...

So what things do you need to consider for your own partnership agreement? You must take legal advice on this, but some of the things that will be included are:

- Who is in the partnership?

- What share each partner holds. Not everyone will have the same share, depending upon the circumstances.

- Who has brought what/put what into the business – resources, money, time.

- Who is responsible for what? Let's say one of you was responsible for sending the VAT paperwork off to the accountant but didn't do it and you were then fined – with a partnership agreement you can show who is at fault.

- What will happen if one of you wants to leave the partnership? You might think that you, and your other partners if there are any, are automatically entitled to buy the share of the partner that leaves, but this is only if that has been agreed and is in writing. If it's not, the partner can sell to whomever they wish. Do you want to then be in business with someone you don't know? Or don't like?

- What happens if one of you dies? Sadly, this sometimes occurs. You need to have an agreement in place to determine what happens in that instance.

Partnership agreements are so important. I can't emphasise enough what damage it can do to your business and personal life if you don't have one. The stress of realising you've lost your investment – or worst case scenario, everything you've worked for – just because you weren't on the ball, and then having to pick up the pieces and start again, is just not worth it. For a few hundred pounds, do it!

And, remember, you must take legal advice to ensure that the agreement is watertight. Never draw up any legal document without getting it checked over and put into lawyer speak where appropriate.

Going into partnership with someone else is something to give great consideration to before you move forwards. When you first dream up an idea, it often seems like a fantastic plan to set up a business in conjunction with someone else – whether it be your best friend, group of friends or family member; and the plusses are obvious. Shared workload, shared commitment, and the chance to work with someone you like and who shares the same values as you do. Why wouldn't you want to do that?

However, a few months down the line, the scenario may well be different. How you react to a friend or family member in a social environment may not be the way you will react to them in a work one. The bad habits which once may have seemed endearing could become increasingly irritating, and their lack of urgency, when you are someone who is a person of action, may result in missed opportunities or a go-slow on production – which is likely to make you resentful, and strain your once tight relationship.

When in business with my ex-husband, we made the mistake of employing my step-father. He was a competent DIY-er, but when it came to working in a workshop, he just wasn't up to the job. My ex agonised for weeks about what to do and finally decided that it wasn't going to work and he would have to let him go.

The resultant fallout was extraordinary. Not only did my step-father take it all very personally, when it was purely a business decision, but my mother got involved too; calling me all the names under the sun, accusing me of neglecting my duties towards my step-father and putting my husband first; the end result being that we haven't spoken since. And that was eleven years ago.

Now, in fairness, we had a strained relationship as it was, and I am sure this was just yet another excuse for her to let off steam and indulge her passion for spite. But, nonetheless, it was a distressing experience both for my ex-husband and my children. And it's one that I hear repeated an awful lot.

I am not saying that you shouldn't go into partnership with friends and family members – plenty of people have, and it has been successful – but for the successes there are an equal, if not a greater, number of instances of failure.

So, if it is something you plan to proceed with, it is even more important that you put an agreement together and that, before you jump into this mammoth undertaking, you talk through how you will deal with any unforeseen problems and issues. How you will communicate when things are difficult, and what the touch paper signal will be – in order that you can head off any bad feeling before it even starts.

Limited company

If you are looking to set up a business and benefit from limited liability then a limited company is likely to be the option for you. However, as I've said before, there is much to consider before you make the final decision – and you MUST take advice from an accountant.

Many people start off as a sole trader and, as the business gets off the ground, change to a limited company status. However, some start from scratch using this structure; for instance, if you are setting up a business that will have many suppliers, or your company image necessitates a more formal company status than sole trader. In my sphere as a consultant working in the education sector, it was important that my companies were incorporated and seen to be set up 'professionally'. For some reason, operating as a sole trader is not seen in that light in certain markets.

As a limited company director, I am separate to my business. I am responsible for running it, for ensuring that it operates in an ethical and legal way, and that all obligations regarding Companies House and other organisations are met. If I don't do these things and the company fails, I run the risk of being banned from running a company in the future. More information on these responsibilities is available on the Companies House website. I strongly advise you to read and digest this information

So, if you have decided to set up your own limited company – how do you go about it? In practice it's very straightforward. No doubt your accountant will offer to do this on your behalf but, being very honest with you, they will charge you a relatively significant sum of money – a couple of hundred pounds plus the formation charge – for something that you can do yourself.

You can either register directly through Companies House, or you can find a formation agent online who will register the company at Companies House for you. I am not very good with forms, as you know, and tried the Companies House route to start with. After having the forms returned twice, I decided to give someone else the job of doing it and found an agent.

The first thing you need to do is to check that the company name you would like is available. You can check this online either with Companies House WebChecker or through a formation agent, if you decide to go down that route. The Companies House database will show you the names of all companies, past and present, and you can then see whether your proposed name is already listed. If so, you may need to consider a different one.

Sometimes people are absolutely set on a particular name and see that someone else has beaten them to it but the company is now dissolved. In some instances, Companies House will let you use the name again but I would be very cautious about doing this. You have absolutely no idea what the previous directors of this company did; what they traded, how they traded, what state they left the company in, what the reputation of the company was before it was dissolved, who they owed money to, what customers thought of them etc. Personally, I would never consider taking on a dissolved company name but it is, of course, your choice. Think very carefully before opting for this and *take independent advice* before making the final decision.

When you have checked your company name and found that it's available, now you can go ahead and register. Exciting times! At time of writing – May 2014 – it costs £15 to do this online, £40 by post, and £100 for a same day service through Companies House. However, online formation agents can be cheaper. Some even offer the service free. But before you immediately opt for the free service, take a step back. A lesson in life as we all know is that nothing is free! There is always a catch! This is no exception.

When you search for formation agents and look at their websites, you will see that most offer a range of packages – from the free to the relatively expensive. Some offer a service that, in my opinion, is really not worth it – free or not. What you are looking for is registration of your company with a copy of the incorporation certificate. Emailed or posted, it makes little difference – unless you want a nicely printed version on card, in which case do pay the extra money they will charge. Of course, you could just print it out yourself on card at home... Remember to save the emailed version into your documents in case you ever need another copy.

The free service invariably comes with an introduction to an accountant, a free bank account and other such offers. Now yes, this sounds great, but in practice I am sure that you would rather choose all of this yourself. It's important to be sure that you have the right accountant – one that you trust and can get on with – and the same with a bank manager.

However, if you are happy to ignore the constant telephone calls, or to tell them that you don't require their services after all, then by all means go with the free option. I would imagine that there is a clause in the agreement that says you must use these services for a minimum period – how else can the formation agent make their commission on the introductions, which is what enables them to offer you a free company registration that we all know costs a minimum of £15? So make sure that you read the small print before you sign or agree to anything.

Personally, I'd happily pay the £15 to an agent and let them have the hassle of getting the paperwork right without the extras they offer.

When you start to complete the online forms, they will ask a series of questions about the company, its directors and shareholdings. Assuming that your company is straightforward and able to use model Articles of Association (details of how the company is going to be run) then online is easy. If not, take advice and proceed in the way that your advisor recommends.

Questions you will be asked will include:

- The company's name and registered address.

- The names of all directors – you must have at least one.

- The names of all shareholders – you must have at least one.

- Details of the company's shares (Memorandum of Association).

- The rules of how the company will be run (Articles of Association).

Let's go through these one at a time.

Name and registered address

Most directors will use their accountant or lawyer's address, or their trading premises if they have one, as their registered address. As I have already mentioned, as a director, your personal address will also be required by Companies House, but it will only be visible on a paid for, more detailed check by anyone who wants to know more about the company and its directors. A brief check of any company will always give the registered address details. Therefore, if you want to keep work and home separate, using a different registered address makes sense.

Names of all directors

All directors' names must be registered. You will need a minimum of one director. Most micro businesses (under five employees) have one director, and a lot of start-ups begin with just one. Having said that, there is no law saying you can't have more than one – it's whatever suits you and your business. If you take on more directors at any point, you MUST advise Companies House immediately; as with any other changes.

Names of all shareholders

All shareholders' names must be registered. You will need a minimum of one shareholder. Of course, the likelihood is that it will be you as the director. However, if you have an investor, or a silent partner, then this person must also be registered. This then brings into play the issue of shareholder agreements and who is entitled to what percentage of the business. You MUST take advice on this, and speak to an accountant and/or a lawyer who will draw up the relevant documentation. If you release more shares, and therefore bring in a new shareholder/s, you must notify Companies House.

Details of the company's shares – Memorandum of Association

Assuming you have a standard company structure and set up, using an online formation agent will be fine. They will ask the questions necessary to ensure that the correctly completed Memorandum of Association is sent with your company incorporation application. They will also send you a copy for your records.

If, having taken advice when you were considering the correct legal structure for your company, it was decided that your company was not relatively straightforward, then using an expert to draft this is your only option. Please do not go against any professional advice given in this area.

If you release more shares, and therefore bring in a new shareholder/s, you must notify Companies House by sending in an updated Memorandum of Association.

The rules of how the company will be run – Articles of Association

Again, assuming that your company structure and set up is straightforward, this is something you can do online, and the formation agent will ask you the relevant questions to ensure that they send the correctly worded Articles of Association to Companies House. You will receive a copy for your records.

However, if again, having taken advice when you were considering the correct legal structure for your company, it was decided that your company was not relatively straightforward, then using an expert to draft this is your only option. Please do not go against any professional advice given in this area.

If you change the way that your company is run, you must notify Companies House by sending in an updated Articles of Association.

Once you have entered all the information, the formation agent's site will give you an overview of what you have given them before you press the button to incorporate your company. They will then handle the paperwork for you and, depending upon the package you have chosen, you will receive your incorporation paperwork and other documentation shortly thereafter. Your accountant and bank will both need copies of the incorporation certificate.

Once you are a company director, you will be required to send in annual returns confirming that the details Companies House holds on your company are correct. This includes directors' names and addresses, and the same for shareholders, as well as whether the company has traded.

Your accountant, assuming you have appointed one, will do all of this for you and will include the cost in your yearly charge. Some people will complete the returns themselves each year, but I have always entrusted this to my accountant. Whilst I am relatively good at remembering to do things, this isn't a deadline that you want to miss. If the information isn't sent in on time, the company will be subject to a fine and – ultimately – could be struck from the register. Not good.

If the company hasn't traded in the financial year, then it is classed as dormant. There is a box on the annual return that can be ticked to show this. You then send the document back to Companies House and they will update their records accordingly.

If the company has traded, then you will also need to send in its yearly accounts along with the return.

If you move house or office, you must advise Companies House – particularly if you have not appointed an accountant to handle the return on your behalf, and all correspondence is sent to your home or office address. If the forms are either not returned to Companies House, or returned marked 'Gone away' or 'Not at this address', then the wheels will be put in motion and, ultimately, the company can be struck off. Can you imagine yourself still merrily trading away without realising that this has happened? It can lead to all sorts of problems.

Unlike operating as a sole trader when you must notify HMRC yourself once you start trading, they are notified automatically when you register a limited company. You will then receive the relevant paperwork through the post, with all of the reference numbers and things that you must do – including the company's assumed tax year and year end. This can be changed to suit your trading plans but, again, HMRC must be notified. You can't just change it yourself and not tell them. If you have appointed an accountant, they will do all of this on your behalf, and will send you the forms to sign that advise HMRC that they are your representatives.

Something to be aware of when running a limited company is that you have to write the company details on all documentation, including your website, headed paper, invoices and emails. You must write:

ABC Limited

Registered as a limited company in England and Wales
(or Scotland or N Ireland where appropriate)

Company number

Registered office address.

You are at risk of a hefty fine if you don't have this information on anything that clients and suppliers come into contact with, so please ensure that, if you haven't already done it, you do it now!

Setting up a limited company is not something to undertake lightly, and you must be fully informed of all the ramifications and responsibilities before you go ahead. I have said it many times, and will continue to do so – take advice before making this decision.

SECTION THREE: YOUR DETAILS
Key personnel

Whilst planning your business, you will have been thinking not just about your idea, but also about those people involved in making it happen. You will have read the previous chapters about skills and talents and identified areas where you, as the architect of this fabulous business, need no help or some help. This section is where you write all this information down and use it to convince the reader – or investor – why you are the person to make this happen. What they are looking for is evidence of the experience, qualifications and general passion that you have. After all, there is little point in setting up a business in an area you know nothing about. I have heard precious few stories of success about people starting a company that they have no experience of. You have nothing to draw on, no terms of reference for problems or challenges.

Of course, it might be that you are running the business alongside someone who DOES have that experience – in which case, their information must be listed in the plan so that an overall view can be taken.

A few pointers for this section:

Position

What can you call yourself when you are setting up your own business? It's your company. You can be whoever you want to be. You can choose whichever title gives you the most confidence. However, a couple of pieces of advice:

Firstly, Chief Executive Officer (CEO) seems to be a popular choice at the moment. I've no idea why. Really this is meant for those running a PLC (public limited company) or a large limited company with a board of directors and shareholders, not those running a one-woman band If you want to use that term then, of course, it's your choice, but it's not strictly correct.

Secondly, don't use the term 'manager'. You aren't the manager. You're the owner. So make sure that you use the term that correctly describes your role in the business. Remember that you will be judged on this when you meet people – prospective clients, suppliers, bank managers, other businesspeople. Rightly or wrongly. So make sure that you adequately represent yourself without going overboard.

I describe myself as Managing Director, which is what I am. If I took on a business partner then they would be a director too, and that would be reflected in their title. Or if I took on an employee who was in charge of running the business on a day to day basis, then their title would reflect that.

Responsibilities

What do you do on a day to day basis in your business? What are your responsibilities both to the business and to your staff/suppliers (where appropriate)? I can guarantee that you will undersell yourself on this part of the plan – we all do; mainly because we have no idea how much we really do! Perhaps write the list as you see it now, then make a note of everything you do in a week, and go back and add what's missing at the end of it. It's likely to be a long list...

If you have a fellow business partner/director then of course you list each other, and your responsibilities, separately. These would also be reflected in your job titles.

Relevant experience and knowledge

What experience or knowledge do you already have that you will be bringing to the business? List anything that's relevant but don't just throw anything in. Make sure that it does apply. You may have worked in the industry before; studied the subject for years; or perhaps worked in a complementary area that has some crossovers.

Previous employment

This section is where you list previous employment that is both relevant and also indicative of other skills that will be useful in the business. Make sure you tease out the points that will show you off to your best in terms of this new business venture.

Key skills

This is a chance to go back to the previous chapters where we looked at skills, and to demonstrate which of those key skills are useful here. Think about what the business needs from you. What can you bring to it? What are your strengths? Don't just write a bland list – display how they will benefit the business and your plans.

This section needs to be replicated for any business partners/fellow directors that you may have.

Other key personnel

This section is for shareholders. Are you bringing someone into the business who is going to offer either money or other resources to help get it off the ground? Are you bringing someone on board who is an expert in this field and is going to work as an advisor to both you and the business? If so, this is where they can shine. Show how their contribution will make a real difference to the business and its plans.

CASE STUDY

Jade Stoner

Jade runs Success Boutique, a business and professional development hub offering resources to help business owners, start ups, freelancers and entrepreneurs achieve and sustain success. Jade is 27 and lives with her seven-year-old son in Essex, UK.

I launched Success Boutique in January 2014, but prior to that I had been running business to business networking exhibitions in East London and Essex called Love Business Expo. Success Boutique is following on from the ethos of Love Business Expo, to inspire, motivate and connect those in business, but changing the format from exhibitions to a website, and adding in a personal development element. I have wanted to build a personal/professional development resource for many years but lacked the confidence and the capital. I decided to launch the business exhibitions first because they were the easiest to start on a tight budget with good profit margins. More importantly, I knew I would gain the confidence and knowledge needed to pursue my dream. I was approved for a Start Up Loan at the end of 2013, and that felt like a breath of fresh air. More than the money itself, it gave me renewed confidence in my business and myself because these companies believed in me. I have been an advocate of personal and professional development since I joined a network marketing company in 2010. It opened my mind to a whole new way of thinking and having a passion for business also, I quickly realised the benefit and power the two had when used in unison. Personal development has been around since the beginning of time and is huge in America, but it is still a very new concept here in the UK and I believe it is the beginning of something very special. I am not yet where I want to be, but I know I am on my way. Success to me means being financially free and having choices in life without worrying how much it all costs and being able to provide for myself and my family. I've heard so many people say they choose not to have any more children because of the costs. I've always wanted a big family and I refuse to let money be the decider in whether or not that happens.

Website: www.successboutique.co.uk

Chapter 7:
Your business – The Vision

SECTION FOUR: YOUR VISION

When you set up a business it's because you have a vision. Sight of something that you think will make a difference, not only to other people's lives but to yours too. It's an exciting journey.

This part of the business plan is all about that vision – what will the business do, what are its goals and what makes it different? It's a chance for you to really lay out on paper what it is about this idea that has lit your passion, and how it can be made to happen.

What will the business do?

We have already looked at the mission statement for your business, which is a short and succinct definition of its activity. This section is designed to allow you to give more detail – to explain what the business will do, who it will interact with, and how you will use the vision to make money.

Use this part of the plan to write some aims – what the business intends to achieve – as well as some information on customers and where the business will sit within the market, i.e. pricing, quality.

Business goals/targets

Part of the vision for your business is looking at its goals – what do you want to happen to it over a given time period? This isn't the same as having business aims. Goals or targets are more tangible; aims are a desired outcome, the dream of where you'd like the business to go.

When you develop your goals, you should have a very specific idea of what you want to achieve and how you will do so, otherwise you can't measure whether your goal has truly been reached. An easy way to do this is to use SMART targets.

Specific

Measured

Achievable

Realistic

Timely.

Each goal should incorporate the above features. For example:

'I want to make enough money to pay the bills' is not a SMART target. It is neither specific nor measured (what is enough money?); we don't know if it's achievable or realistic because we don't know how much money the company needs to make; and we also don't know if it's timely as no time limit has been set.

A better target would be:

'I want to bring in sales of £15000 in the first year of trading.' It is specific – we have a stated amount of money; measurable – again, we know the figures; achievable and realistic – we would be able to check that by looking at the figures in the back of the business plan; and timely – there's a timeframe: in the first year of trading.

A popular first year goal is often that a company wants to break even. There is a school of thought that says a business may well take two or three years to start making a profit and that you shouldn't take a salary out in the first year. In my opinion, and with my personal circumstances, that's not good enough. As a single mum with no other income, I couldn't be in a position where I took no salary from the business I was working in. That may work for those who have another income coming into their household, but for single mums it's going to be a non-starter. Therefore, you would certainly want your business to at least break even in its first year. That way you would be able to take an income, and not be left with any debts.

As the business grows of course, you can start to look at the sort of profit you might be able to make as a goal, or perhaps expansion into other geographical areas, taking on staff, developing new products etc.

When writing the three- to five-year goals, let this be a chance to allow your mind to wander. As it stands at present, you have no idea what will really happen in year one, let alone in years three to five. But it is your vision. It's your hope of what might happen, so write it down. Remember that this is a living document, and something to be referred back to on a regular basis. I can assure you that there will be moments when you wonder what you are doing this all for – and to be able to read something you wrote at the start of this fascinating journey about what you would like to achieve in the long term is a real motivator.

What makes the business different?

Let's not pretend – there are a lot of businesses out there; all fighting for their own share of the market they operate in. The only way that the strong will survive and prosper is to be different. Unique. To stand out as desirable. So, you need to think about how you will develop that company. What is it about your offer that makes your company desirable?

The business plan asks you to list your products and services and then their features and benefits. Successful sales people know that to get orders, you sell on the benefits not the features.

- A feature is 'a distinctive characteristic of a good or service that sets it apart from similar items'.

- A benefit is 'the gain, value or advantage the customer will receive by using a product or service'.

To use my favourite example, I am now holding up my trusty pen. You, of course, can't see it but believe me, I am.

So. This is my trusty pen. The ink is black (the feature) which means that my writing can be seen clearly when I write (the benefit).

This is my trusty pen. I can write upside down with it (the feature) which means that when I am in space – where I often go – and am upside down, I can still carry on writing my latest business plan (the benefit).

This is my trusty pen. The ink is waterproof (the feature) which means that when I am submerged in the bath – which I am constantly – I can carry on writing my latest business plan and the words will be visible for all to see (the benefit). Of course, the paper will have dissolved but the ink will still be there. Perhaps that's a potential business diversification...

Does that make sense? Can you see how selling the benefit to the customer rather than the feature would encourage them to buy – and, even more importantly, start to show how your product/service is different to others?

You are looking for what makes your offer unique compared to your competitors.

This leads to your Unique Selling Point (USP). What is it about your company overall that makes you different? Lots of people sell on quality or customer service. These are two great USPs to develop. Innovation is another. You might want to sit down with a friend and talk through your business with them to see what comes out if you are struggling to identify one area. Sometimes you can be a little too close to the problem to see the solution.

Legal and insurance requirements

The law and insurance tend to be areas that people don't always think about until it's too late – and you don't ever want to be in that situation. So what laws will apply to you, and what legal protection do you need to put in place to protect both your-self and your business?

As always, it is best to take advice on these issues, but for general consideration let's look at the following:

- Are there specific laws that apply to your profession? Professions that instantly spring to mind are catering, sport, health, beauty.

- What licences and registrations do you need?

- As a retailer, there are laws that will apply to products and services you sell, including the Sale of Goods Act 1979 and others.

- You will also need to consider the laws that apply to you when you let someone through the doors of your retail outlet.

- If you are going to employ someone, you will need to investigate employment laws, as well as those surrounding Health and Safety.

- To protect yourself and your business, you will require contracts for sales (if necessary), plus obviously for any staff you may employ.

From an insurance point of view, what will you need to consider?

- If you use your personal car for business use, you will need to update your insurer.

- If you use part of your home for business, you will need to update your insurer.

- Do you need insurance for your particular business, e.g. consultancy/advice services?

- Insurance for your business assets and premises.

Of course, there are many other scenarios in which you will require legal and insurance protection, so please ensure that you take advice. A lawyer's advice is invaluable if you have to draw up specific documents, and an insurance broker will always discuss any requirements with you.

Remember that when it comes to taking advice, you get what you pay for. Ensure too that you factor the cost of any professional help and advice into your start-up costs.

It doesn't pay to take shortcuts when it comes to legal and insurance issues. You don't want to be caught out on something really small that can become something really big and potentially devastating for your business. Start as you mean to carry on – making sensible decisions.

And remember, as a company director it is your job to make sure that the company adheres to the law – not knowing is not a defence.

CASE STUDY

Chris Farren

Chris Farren is a 27-year-old singer/songwriter based in Naples, Florida. He also tours with his band Fake Problems.

My mum has been working hard my whole life. She's always had a career of some sort; it's just the way it's always been. She's always made time for me and I never felt like I was coming in second to anything. She has set the example of working hard and always staying busy. I've learned to always keep going and to evolve and adapt as the people and circumstances around me change. To keep moving through failures and not let anything negative weigh too heavily on me. My goal is to reach a point in my career where I feel a more consistent sense of confidence and creativity. I'll be successful just by maintaining an exciting life in a career or work that is creatively fulfilling, shared with the people I love.

Website: www.chrisfarren.com

Chapter 8:
Your business – Marketing

SECTION 5: MARKETING

If you have a creative mind then the marketing part of your business plan could well appeal to you. It's an opportunity to let your thoughts run wild and to explore all sorts of possibilities not necessarily given to you in other parts of the plan.

I love exploring what my customers are looking for, what gaps my competitors are leaving wide open, and how I can exploit them in the most creative way possible. It's a chance to really get my teeth into a problem that needs solving – and I adore the challenge! Sometimes you win, sometimes you don't, but until you do the research, and then try the results out on the market, you don't know what your business is capable of.

Customer research

I am always slightly bemused by people who tell me that they are progressing nicely with their plans to set up a business without having researched the need for it first. For one, it seems to be a rather arrogant view, and two? It's likely to be a waste of their time. And money.

My ex-husband and I did exactly the same. It was arrogant. And it did fail. We had been moving along nicely with our first business; it was doing really well and we were getting some fabulous clients on board. Then one day my ex-husband showed me a brochure that had come through from one of the smaller timber merchants, with pictures of some beautiful, naturally coloured woods. Deep reds, shocking oranges; the colours were extraordinarily vibrant.

I was instantly hooked, as was he. We were sure that there must be an opportunity for us to use these in our business. However, they were as costly as they were dazzling and there was no way that our average client would be able to afford a piece of furniture solely made out of these woods, even if our average client was pretty wealthy. The cost was prohibitive.

We put our thinking caps on and a few weeks later thought we had the answer. We would use leather and these timbers together. That way we could still design a beautiful piece of furniture and use the wood at the same time. Height of sophistication and design taste.

Except, of course, that it wasn't. Because although the piece we made looked beautiful, it took forever to cover with the leather (which cost an arm and a leg) and, crucially, – no one wanted it. Even though we'd invested a lot of money into the prototype, and the setting up of the new company.

We were ahead of our time. We were innovative at a time when people wanted traditional luxury not cutting edge. We were arrogant because we didn't actually ask the people we thought would be interested in buying the product – we just assumed. Assumption is the mother of all cock-ups, so the saying goes. In my experience, I would concur.

Market research does not consist of asking your best friend or your mum if they would buy your product or service. It doesn't consist of inviting a couple of mates round on a Friday evening and getting their opinion over a glass or three of wine. It doesn't even consist of asking the mums at playgroup or the school gates what they think. Similarly it doesn't involve thinking that because you'd like it, everyone else would too. None of these are classed as proper, bona fide research. None of them are unbiased. These people will all tell you what a great idea it is – 'Wow, you're so brave/clever/amazing!' – because they love you and want you to be successful. That isn't proper research. That's asking for vindication of your plans, with a bit of moral support thrown in for good luck.

If you want to plan your business on the back of this kind of research then carry on, but no investor worth his or her salt is going to be interested in working with you if you can't justify your marketing decisions – and a bank manager will pick you up on it too.

Proper research entails sitting down and thinking very carefully about who your potential customers might be – and then finding them to ask lots of questions, give them samples of your product or service and get their feedback. It involves looking at your competitors and seeing what they do that's good, and what they do that's not so good – and that you can capitalise on and make your USP; as well as your ticket to success.

Can you see why it's so important?

So, how do you start undertaking market research? You've obviously identified a product or service that you think is missing from the market and now you need to see if that is really the case. Do people actually want it and, crucially, will people pay for it?

1. Firm up your offer

You need to be clear about your offer. It's very easy to have a great idea and to develop it, but not then be able to articulate what it is or what benefits it will bring to the consumer. Look back at the features and benefits section and compile half a dozen for each product or service that you are offering. If you aren't clear about what you are selling, how do you expect your client to be clear about whether they need it or not?

2. Decide who your customer is

Again, it's easy to be general about who your customer is but you need to know definitively who they are. Down to their shoe size. You have to be the expert on all things to do with your business, and no aspect more than who your customer is. You can drill down and down on this area until you almost know everything there is to know about them. Supermarkets are expert at this – think loyalty cards.

Don't just say that your target market is women aged 18-25. What else do you know about them? In what geographical area do they live? What car do they drive? What TV programmes do they watch? What hobbies do they have? What job do they do? The more you know about them, the more you can tailor your offer, and the easier it is to find them when conducting a marketing campaign towards them.

3. Take your product to your customer

Your potential customers will need to see your product, or experience your service. If it's a product, they will want to handle it; smell it, touch it, feel it. It will be an experience. And that's what you want. You need their feedback on every aspect of the product so that you can refine it further to ensure that every part, however little, is perfect.

If it's a service, they will want to experience it. Again, this is crucial as you need feedback on all aspects of the offer.

4. Ask them questions

Don't just ask the obvious questions: Do you like it? What would you pay? Although these are, of course, crucial questions, there are so many more things you want to know. What do you think of the packaging? Of the name? Of the fragrance/flavour/colour? What other fragrances/flavours/colours would you like? Where would you expect to buy this? How would you expect it to be sold to you? How would you expect it to make you feel? How does it make you feel? Is it something you would want to buy more than once? How long would you expect it to last? Does it solve the problem I've identified (the key question!)? I could go on.

Do you see the permutations of question? How you can ask one question but it should lead on to another? That you want to explore every possible avenue whilst you have these customers in front of you?

Make sure that you have a selection of closed and open questions ready. Some that need only a brief yes or no, and others that require more detail.

PS – don't forget to get their contact details for when your product/service is ready to go on sale. These could well be your first customers!

5. Collate their answers

The information you have collected is gold dust. It's what will enable you to develop your product/service further into something that customers will want to buy. Collate onto a spreadsheet and highlight any consistent points. Be open minded. Remember that these people are becoming your product experts.

6. Refine your offer

Use the information raised by your test group and ensure that you act on every point that's been made. Nothing should be missed or ignored. Go back to the drawing board and make changes where recommended. Remember that your feelings aren't important – you aren't buying the product, your customer is. Try to keep emotion out of product development as much as you can.

7. Ask them more questions

Take the revised product/service back to the group, along with the original, and see what they think this time round. Ask more questions. Which do you prefer? What else could we improve? Does it now completely solve the problem I identified? Have we got the fragrance/taste/colour right this time? Do you like the new packaging? What about the name? Where else would you like to be able to purchase the item?

Be open with your questions. Don't avoid asking a question because you don't want to hear the answer. This is all good stuff and vital to your business development.

8. Finalise your offer

Now you can take all of this information back again and finalise your product/ service. Now you know that you have something customers will want to buy. If it's a product, you know that they like the smell/taste/colour; the name; how it makes them feel. You know that they think it solves the problem you identified in the market, and they like the price. They've even identified where and how they'd like to purchase.

So, now it's just down to you to get producing or selling your service.

I've used focus groups for the market research scenario above but you can use other forms of research – online questionnaires (try Survey Monkey) or one to one questionnaires in person; online research; reading relevant reports and articles etc. You will know how to find your customers best; after all, you're the expert in the field. Use your imagination, and let your creativity run wild.

Competitor research

As important as customer research is competitor research. That might surprise you but, quite frankly, taking a start-up into a new market with no idea of who else is out there is akin to walking in the woods in the pitch dark with no torch. Not only have you no idea who you might bump into or what you might fall into, but you've no idea what you'll do if – when – you do.

It's vital to know who is competing against you, and their strengths and weaknesses, so that you can develop your business in response. You need to know everything about them, from their pricing structure to their product/service line, from their suppliers to their customer service policy. Not only do you need to be the expert in your business, you need to be the expert in theirs too.

When I set up my first business with my ex-husband, I knew nothing about premium furniture makers. However, I made it my business to get to know everything there was to know, and within a short space of time I did.

I pored over magazines and brochures; visited showrooms and timber merchants. I made friends with interior designers and picked the brains of carpenters and cabinetmakers alike. I wanted to know everything I needed to know, and to find out what I needed to know that I didn't know I needed to know! My thirst for knowledge was endless.

Then I rang half a dozen companies who I thought would be our closest competitors, both geographically and directly. I pretended to be a potential customer and wrote copious notes, from how they answered the phone and how quickly, to how friendly they were and what information they gave me. I asked for brochures and particular product information and wrote notes on how quickly everything arrived, and in what state. What was their brochure like? What was their website like? Then I emailed three of them to arrange an appointment, and wrote notes on how quickly they responded to my email and how professional their replies were.

When the three visited my house, I told them I was looking for some furniture for a dining room and they measured up for a small bookcase. I wrote notes on what they were like when they came to my house – how they were dressed, how friendly they were, what their van was like and what information they asked me for. And finally, what the resultant drawings were like – and how much they charged me for them, as well as for the piece itself and how quickly they could turn it around for me.

You are probably thinking it's a bit harsh, pretending to be a potential client. No, it isn't. It's business. It gave me all the information I needed to finalise our own offer, and allowed me to examine other companies' strengths (how were they so good in particular areas, for instance?) and their weaknesses (something for us to exploit to our advantage). It also gave me a really good indication of what other companies charged, what their customer service offer was like, and whether they really delivered what they promised.

And guess what? I know that they did exactly the same to us when we had been in business for a while. It got to the point where we could tell which calls were genuine and which weren't, but everyone got the same service and courtesies; whether or not we were going to get some business from them.

It makes sense to check out the competition! If you don't, you don't develop. If you don't develop, you stand still. And if you stand still, your competitors move straight past you. More fool you.

Pricing

There are many ways of calculating your prices – some are really ma... some aren't. There are also a few basic rules that apply however you may come your ultimate pricing decision:

- Always ensure you cover your costs.

- Always ensure that you make a profit.

- Always ensure that your price is consistent with your branding message.

Ensuring that you cover your costs might sound like an obvious point. However, I have come across a few businesses over the years that have failed due precisely to the fact that they haven't.

The owner would run a small, micro business that operated predominantly in a local area – meaning that he or she knew all of the customers very well. This often meant that they were, or became, friends. That's always a problem because friends, as with family, often expect special treatment and discounted prices. I have no idea why they think like this – surely as a friend or family member, you not only want the business to succeed even more than you might ordinarily, but you see the value of it and are prepared to pay for what you want – but they do. Personally I think that families, friends and businesses in general don't mix and are best avoided. But that's another conversation.

Over time, with the discounts and special favours that the friends required in order to purchase items, the business owners would find that, not only were they run ragged with very little spare time, but they weren't making enough money to cover their costs. In one case, I know of a business owner who was funding the business himself to keep it going. Instead of seeing that the business was viable because it obviously had something that people wanted to buy (even though these particular customers wanted huge discounts), the owners carried on trading in the same rut; selling to people who didn't value what they had, rather than finding new customers who would.

All three of the businesses that came to mind for me to tell you that story, failed.

And it's a shame because they didn't need to.

You must make sure that you have calculated your prices so that they cover your costs; ALL of your costs. So that includes your time – whether making items or collecting the resources and materials needed in order to make the items. Everything must be costed and calculated; and tossed into the pricing pot.

Always ensure that you make a profit. Again, that might seem obvious but it isn't necessarily.

When you first set up a business, you may well lack the confidence to sell properly. That's not unusual. It takes a lot of guts to go out there and sell something, particularly if it's something you've made yourself, so there is an element of nerves and not being confident about your price. However, if you aren't confident about it – how can your customers be confident?

You must ensure, for the growth of your business, that you have factored in an element of profit. Assuming you have already worked in the industry, you will know – or you will know someone who knows – the accepted profit margins of that market. All business areas have an accepted margin. If you don't, then you need to consider what would be acceptable for your own business. This is where your bank manager or accountant's advice would be extremely useful.

All businesses need to be able to grow, and they can't without profit. Profit is the part that enables you to update your machinery; take on new employees; engage in a marketing campaign; move to bigger premises; expand to a new geographical area; develop a new product. Pay yourself more money! Without it, you might as well accept that you will just bumble along from day to day without being able to grow your dreams beyond germination of that initial seed of an idea.

Branding

Ensuring that your price fits with your branding message is also very important. Branding and price sit hand in hand. Charging a high price but having an obviously homemade logo and website are incongruous. The two must match.

If you are going to go mass market, and therefore price on the cheaper side, then there is little point investing in glossy brochures and a swish website. As long as your marketing is well thought through and fit for purpose, as well as fluent in design, then customers will be attracted to your company. However, if you are going to charge at the top end and attract those with money, you need to market accordingly. Everything you do has to be top end; from business cards through to your customer service. Nothing can be dropped, a beat can't be missed. Clients who are paying good money will expect an excellent service. The minute you don't deliver, you lose them.

A good example of this would be in fashion retail. There are the shops at the bottom end; clothes piled high, priced cheaply with difficult to navigate aisles. We expect to queue for a while to pay, and that we may not have the quality we'd like. The advertising isn't glossy but it serves its purpose. We get what we pay for.

Then there are the shops sitting in the middle in terms of pricing. The clothes are generally of a good quality; service is quicker and marketing is glossier. The stores are less cluttered but still difficult to get round quickly. We don't expect to buy something and for it to fall apart or lose its shape within a week or two, but similarly we don't expect it to last forever.

At the top end would be a designer label. We expect to pay top prices but we get top quality. The marketing is glossy and chic, as are the stores. Few items are displayed, allowing a seamless journey around the racks, and a glass of champagne is proffered as we walk through the door.

Use these examples to think about your branding. Where would your business fit? How can you demonstrate this through your marketing and the overall purchasing experience? Even online there are ways that you can differentiate. And it all adds to your USP.

You must also organise a logo and corporate colours, as well as a professional website to show off your company. When I say professional, I don't mean spending lots of money that you don't have at the beginning on a site – I mean it must look professional, and read as thought it's been written by a professional. Even if it hasn't!

Paying for a well-designed logo is money well-spent. Please resist the temptation to design your own, unless you are a designer. It really will catch you out in the long term and, at some point, you'll have to go through a rebranding exercise which is costly and disruptive. Far better to invest up front – make this one of the few things you need to spend a chunk of money on – and have something to be proud of, and that transmits your message properly.

Promotion, advertising and PR

A common misconception about marketing is that it's just about advertising. Wrong! Marketing is so much more, as we've already demonstrated. It's about perception, attraction – and as much about money as the financials at the back of the plan. Without marketing, you have no business.

So, how are you going to use the work you've done so far to attract customers and clients to your new business when they have so much choice out there? This is where promotion, advertising and PR come in.

Promotion

Promotion is a really useful marketing tool but it shouldn't be seen as the only one, nor used in isolation. It can range from free merchandise (pens, hats etc) to promotional offers such as Buy One Get One Free (BOGOF). Competitions and giveaways can also be part of a promotional campaign. Used as part of an overall marketing strategy, promotion is very effective, but it shouldn't be overused; particularly if part of the promotion is discounted items. Customers can get too used to discounts and this starts to devalue the product and, ultimately, the company.

One only needs to think about sofa companies and double-glazing manufacturers/installers, with their continual sales and promotional discounts advertised on TV, to see the damage that can be done. It does come to a point where the consumer can't really decide whether the promotion is the real price or it's all an elaborate charade.

Advertising

Advertising is everywhere. There are statistics showing that we are exposed to a staggering amount of ads each day – consciously and subconsciously – and that's not likely to change any time soon. Consumers are becoming a little jaded by advertising these days, and who can blame them? This means that the company that can come up with an innovative and creative campaign is certain of a round of applause, and new customers to boot.

Alongside the traditional print advertising, you can use broadcast, guerrilla, outdoor, direct-mail, Point of Sale (POS), mobile phone and online channels – to name but a few. It's a minefield out there, people, so be sure that when you take the time out to speak to your potential customers during your market research phase, you also make sure that you find out which of these would be the most efficient way to reach them.

Of course, the costs and the results are all different and it isn't always a case of the less you pay, the less you receive. You can put together a relatively effective online campaign with good results, compared to the cost of print or broadcast. My recommendation would be to sit down and plan where best you think you can reach your potential clients, and then investigate a campaign that will fit your budget. Don't think that you need lots of money to run advertising and promotional campaigns. You don't, but you do need to focus and use the time you are investing in planning wisely.

Public Relations (PR)

PR is another useful marketing tool but often not used as much as the others, purely due to cost and the assumption that, as a small or micro business, it isn't affordable or appropriate. Wrong on both counts!

I have run five businesses now, and never used a PR agency. Until a month ago. I suddenly realised that if I was going to develop and build on my hard work of the last two and a half years, and capitalise on the fabulous opportunities that had recently come my way, I needed to up my game. And PR was the way forwards.

Now, I'm pretty good at marketing. I worked as a self-employed marketing consultant for a while back in the nineties, and also lectured in it at degree level during my brief teaching career. I have more marketing books than you can shake a stick at (and I've read them!) but I really didn't want to tackle my PR. Why? Out of all the components involved in a successful marketing campaign, this is the one where you can see the least reward for your time if you don't know what you're doing. And I don't. I don't have the contacts, I don't have the time to devote to finding them – and I don't really know where to start. For me, it made sense to employ an expert with a track record to do it for me.

However, for a start-up it's certainly something to have a go at, particularly if you have a good knowledge of local journalists and/or relevant trade press. Press releases can be written and sent out whenever you think there's a great news story to tell, e.g. company/product launch, an industry award, a new large client etc. Local papers often have a business section where they like to feature companies, and sometimes they also have sections for stories that are relevant to women. Both are perfect for single mums.

Social Media

No marketing section would be complete without consideration of social media. Its importance has increased over the last few years and a start-up that neglects this area is not doing itself any favours. This is a chance for potential and current customers to interact with you – and for you to interact right back! If you have a customer base of under 25s, you might as well give up right now if you haven't got a website, Twitter, Facebook, Instagram and other social media accounts set up and ready to go.

First stop is, of course, a website. The shop window and office that is open 24/7, even at Christmas and New Year. However, nowadays a static website just won't impress. Make sure that yours is interactive; so not only does it give the user information, but it encourages them to interact with you through it – asking them to vote on an article, leave a comment, or even tailoring your content to whoever happens to be browsing at the time. Adding video content or podcasts, for instance, are becoming more popular too.

Twitter, Facebook, Instagram, Snapchat and others are all also vital to investigate and act upon where relevant to your customer base. It is expected that you will at least interact through Twitter and Facebook; other forms of social media are often tailored to specific uses and/or demographics so may not always be relevant to every business.

Alongside writing a marketing campaign, start-ups should be writing a social media campaign, and taking the slow but steady advent of everything going online very seriously. Making it easy for customers to shop online, pay online, book online and interact with you online is a given. Don't get this wrong.

CASE STUDY

Peggy Farren

Peggy Farren, now 54, started her business when her son was a teenager, though she was a single mum for most of his life. Peggy is based in Florida, USA. Her son is now 27.

In 2011, I left my job as a photographer and videographer to start my own company as a wedding videography company. It seemed that the demand was high in the competition was very low. I was right about the competition but wrong about the demand. I added photography to my business and it really started taking off. I'm a big believer in keeping track of what is working and what isn't. Over the years I started specialising in family portraits, which continues to be my highest grossing product. Four years ago my business started suffering again with the influx of what felt like one million new photographers so I started a new division within my company called Understand Photography and started offering photography classes. This is becoming a saturated market as well, so now we are bringing our training to the Internet. The challenges I had were the same as any business owner – time and money! I moved in with my parents when my son was 7 years old so I was super lucky to have free babysitters. It was actually easier than when I had a "real" job since most of my work was at home. When I had a traditional job, I was always scrambling for babysitters.

Photography is a great job for a working mother. It's 80% marketing, 10% editing and 10% taking pictures, so most of the work can be done from home. I really believed in the beginning that once I became an established photographer I would not have to work so hard. This is partly true, but as a business owner you have to always have your eyes open for new opportunities.

Website: Avant-Garde Images, Inc. www.naplesportraits.com
Photography Club and Workshops, www.understandphotography

Chapter 9:
Your business – Operations

SECTION SIX: OPERATIONS AND LOGISTICS

The operations side of the business plan looks at the practical things – where you will work from, what resources you need to carry out your work, who you will work with and who will work for you.

Sometimes this is forgotten in the clamour of sourcing finance, putting the final touches to marketing plans and designs, and all of the other exciting stuff. Operations can seem a bit dull and uninspiring at first glance but all of the aspects are so very, very important. These are the practical matters; the wheels on the glamorous machine.

Staff

Start-ups are designed and planned around the owner's skills and experience so, in a large proportion of cases, staff won't necessarily be an immediate consideration.

However, for some businesses, staff will be needed from day one, and so plans must be put in place to source and recruit the right person/people for the job.

Hiring staff is a big decision, and a huge responsibility. Being responsible for your future and your economic stability is one thing, but being responsible for someone else's too? It's scary, believe me. If money is tight one month, you will have to pay them before you pay yourself – and that might mean not being paid at all, or being paid in dribs and drabs. That is the risk you take when employing people. The long term gain can sometimes mean short term pain. Make sure that you are prepared for eventualities of this sort.

I have employed people in the past and it hasn't always been smooth sailing. Finding the right person can be tricky, particularly if you are looking for someone to take over some of your tasks as the business grows. You will have a very definite idea of how things should be done and the person you hire may think differently. As they probably should of course! You aren't looking to hire a clone of yourself – and if you are, you should be thinking very carefully about your motivation for hiring someone. You want someone with fresh ideas who can bring a brand new pair of eyes to your business. Someone who can help to develop and move your company forwards to even bigger and better things.

If you are looking for someone to work alongside you or for you from the start, then the chances are you may already have spoken to a family member or friend and agreed that they will help you. Whilst I am all in favour of working with people you like and trust – on all levels of a business – and see the many plusses that this arrangement brings, I must take the opportunity to expand further on something I have already brought up a couple of times in this book: working with friends and family.

At the start, it seems logical to work with people you know. Setting up a new business is daunting, with lots of unknown factors that can jump out at you and trip you up. Having the support of a friendly face to help you through the difficult times can seem to be the perfect solution, and in many ways it might be. You will have seen them respond well to tricky situations; you have been able to trust them in the past; you know that they are good at their job and, crucially, you like them. These are all great attributes for a member of your team. When you write your person specification (which we will look at shortly), these are the sorts of skills you will be highlighting.

However, take it from me that this can all change – and sometimes not for the better – when you employ someone you know in your business. Suddenly, loyalties may alter, and what seemed like a charming personality quirk can become an irritation beyond measure. A strong headed and willed person who always gets their own way can change very quickly from someone to admire to someone who is potentially confrontational, when that person works for you and you need them to toe the line.

As mentioned, I have employed friends and family and set up businesses with family in the past, and it has never worked out. Maybe it's because I have a very definite view on things and how I expect them to be done. I suspect it's also because I am a kind-hearted, soft-centred soul who is happy to let things bumble along, sometimes overlooking small problems and even fixing them myself unbeknown to the friend or family member. Until something big happens. And then I take decisive action. The decisive action tends to be swift and unremitting – and friends and family don't like that. But when you run a business, and not only their livelihood but yours too rests on making such decisions, it has to be done. Or perhaps I'm just not cut out to work with friends and family, who knows?

Some people are really good at working with those they have loved and liked for many years. They are expert at dealing tactfully and diplomatically with problems and challenges within their friend and family groups, so that everyone wins in the end where possible. And if they don't win, they don't walk away feeling upset or cross – or at least not for long. I suspect that attribute also has links back to how you were raised, and how you interacted with your family – the relationships as you grew up, and the way you were perhaps all treated equally and as part of a big, happy team. If you felt you were all working together towards a common end then you all pulled together.

I didn't grow up like that and think that my singularly focused and completely independent way of working is what hinders me when it comes to hiring people I know. I don't have that history and, whilst I'd love to be able to work like that, my extended family members certainly aren't able to see the world on that level – so working with them is a no-no.

I worked with both my ex-husband and my step-father – as you already know. Neither of these working relationships succeeded. And I have spoken to many people with similarly unfortunate family tales to tell.

However, I have also spoken to many people where setting up a family business has been a huge success, and some have gone on to be relatively large local employers. There are still issues to resolve, as with all families and businesses, but they all pull together for the common purpose and end goals they want to achieve.

Don't think that just because my experiences of working with family and friends haven't worked, yours won't. Remember that until you try you won't know, and you really are the expert on the relationships in your life. If you think it will work then go for it and enjoy the many positives that it will undoubtedly bring! Remember, however, to seek some advice first and ensure that you have a long chat with your friend or family member before they even start; explain that this is a business relationship not a family one, and that any decisions and requests are purely business and nothing personal. Perhaps, similar to the partnership discussions, talk about how you will resolve any problems and gripes between you so that you can work peaceably together for a long time to come. After all, you obviously saw some fabulous skills and qualities in them to warrant employing them in the first place – and it would be a shame to let that all go to waste for the sake of a miscommunication or misunderstanding.

So, when you hire someone, irrespective of whom it may be, there are a number of things to consider:

What will they do?

• Duties.
• Responsibilities.

Is this a full-time or part-time post?

• You don't always have to hire full-time staff, often part-time works really well.

Permanent or temporary?

• Don't think that all staff have to be permanent; they don't. As long as you make it crystal clear at the start that this is a temporary role, you will find plenty of willing applicants. Often suits students.

Could it be filled by a freelancer or sub-contractor as a short term fix?

- Don't go down the route of thinking that if you need someone to work in your business it must be an employee. Lots of microbusinesses work in collaboration with freelancers, giving them the parts of a project that they themselves can't carry out. Ensure that you take out references and see the quality of their work before using them – and take advice regarding contracts etc.

- Using freelancers saves the hassle of employing someone, and the cost of tax and NI contributions. However, the downside is that they may be too busy to always be available to work with you when you need them – so ensure that you have a pool of people you can turn to.

What salary will you pay?

- Per hour, per year?

What benefits/perks will you offer alongside the salary?

- Bonuses, performance payments, Christmas time off, healthcare.

What are the working hours for the role?

What holidays will they be entitled to? And will you offer more?

Can this be a flexible working post? Would it suit job-share?

What skills, qualifications and experience do you require?

Where will they work?

What resources will you need to employ them?

- Desk, phone, chair, mobile phone, PC/laptop, safety equipment etc.

What laws and regulations will apply to this post?

- Including insurance, and health and safety requirements.

Where will you advertise to recruit for this post?

- Printed press, online, locally, nationally, trade press.

Will you expect CV only applications, or will applicants need to complete an application form?

• Who will draw up the application form and send it out?

Who will sift through applications and decide upon who is to be interviewed?

• What are the criteria?

Will you reply to all applicants or only those who are given an interview?

• It is becoming more common not to be advised if you aren't successful in a job application. Personally, I think it's very bad PR but ultimately it's your choice.

What questions will you ask at interview?

• Have a list in front of you and ask the same of everyone. Ensures parity between each candidate and helps you to remember what you want to ask – and what they reply.

Will you expect them to carry out practical tasks at interview? If so, are you going to notify them in advance or tell them at the interview?

• Role play, job-related task?

Will you invite anyone else to help in the interview process? If so, who and why?

• Business partner, colleague.

Will you interview once, face to face, or perhaps have a telephone interview first?

• For a phone based role, this is an invaluable first interview and something I always do.

Will you shortlist applicants after the first round of interviews?

• If so, what will be the criteria for the shortlist?

Will you give unsuccessful applicants feedback?

• Some companies do, some don't.

How will you notify those who are unsuccessful?

• Email, letter, phone.

Once you have made your decision on the successful applicant/s, how quickly do you expect them to start?

• Take into account their notice period – some will have to give a month's notice, others a week. Some, of course, may be unemployed or coming into their first job so may be able to start immediately.

What is your referencing process?

• You MUST take references. Woe betide you if you don't and the candidate then doesn't work out as you might have hoped. The only person to blame is yourself!

• How many will you take? And from whom? Be careful of those candidates who have obviously worked but only give personal references. Why?

How long is your probation period going to be?

• Average three months but reviewed each month. You make the decision.

Who will write and put together your letter of appointment and employment contracts?

• You can buy employment contracts online, or ask a lawyer to draw one up on your behalf. A worthwhile expense – and a legal must-have.

What will happen on their first day?

• What will you do with them? Will you spend the day with them? Will you ask someone else to do this? Are there tasks they need to learn immediately? Plan this out.

How will you gather the information you need to have not only as their employer, i.e. name, address, next of kin etc, but also pay roll information including P45?

- Draw up a new starter form. Send to your accountant or whoever does your payroll. File a copy in your office, in a locked cabinet.

Who will ensure that their details are set up on your system for pay and tax/NI deductions?

- As above. Send to your accountant.

Assuming you have a probation period, what are the dates for reviews?

- Set these in the first couple of days and diarise.

Who will put together the paperwork for these reviews?

- It's quite easy to find pro-forma probation paperwork online and then adapt to your needs.

What are the criteria for passing each stage of the probation?

Who will send out the passing probation paperwork? Who will send out the failing probation paperwork, if necessary?

- Likely to be you! Ensure it's diarised to do.

What is your disciplinary procedure?

- Take advice on this. It's a legal requirement that your employee knows the disciplinary procedure, and you can be fined for not having one in place.

Who will ensure it is carried out properly and within the law?

- Your responsibility! Take it seriously.

How will you assess that the entire recruitment process has been carried out effectively and efficiently, and where you need to improve? Ensure that improvements are made for next time.

• Review what went well and what didn't. Assuming your hire worked out well, ask for their feedback on the process, and implement for next time.

Wow. That's a lot of things to think about just to hire someone, I'm sure you will agree! However, each of these stages is vital and must be adhered to where appropriate. Miss one out at your peril. Some, if missed, will just make the recruitment process a little more difficult, whilst others could potentially lead to legal problems – which you want to avoid at all costs.

So, how can you catch some of these in one fell swoop? A person specification and job specification are good starts. Both will enable you not only to gain clarity on what you are looking for and what role the person will need to fulfil, but will also help to ensure that the right applicants apply. There is nothing worse than writing a vague advertisement and not being entirely clear in your mind what you need, and then being inundated with applications that are not what you are looking for. A waste of everyone's time.

Hiring someone is a great feeling – proof that your business idea is actually going somewhere. But it is also fraught with potential potholes. Ensure that every step is taken with care and consideration – and legal advice. There is no excuse for making a mistake where the law is concerned. Ignorance is not accepted as a reason. If you are going to be responsible enough to run a business then you MUST be responsible enough to get the recruitment, and employment part, right. If you don't think you can cope with hiring staff, then don't. Use freelancers instead; much more flexibility and less stress (in some ways at least). There are more and more people setting up as freelancers at the moment, particularly in the professions, and you can find some top-notch people to work in your team who you certainly wouldn't be able to afford as permanent members of staff, but you could as freelancers. Worth exploring!

It's unforgiveable to mess up someone else's life, especially their financial security, just because you can't get a handle on employing them. Don't take this kind of decision lightly, and ensure you've thought it all through down to the most minute of detail before you take the leap.

Suppliers

Taking on suppliers is just like taking on staff. They are both an integral part of your business success and it is hugely important to get them right. Suppliers are the lifeblood of your company if you are manufacturing products and they really can determine whether you do well or not. Therefore, it's vital to source the right supplier, and to ensure that you treat them properly in order to get top-notch service and quality, and a little extra help and support when you need it.

I always recommend that when sourcing suppliers, you interview them just as you would a potential employee. Obviously you aren't going to get them to fill in an application form or send in a CV, but you are interested in knowing everything about them and their products. You want to know how they can support your business in order that you can achieve your dreams. If they can't, then they aren't the right supplier for you.

So what are you looking for?

Quality of product.

Range of product.

Ability to send items quickly or urgently if you are in need.
Despite the best laid plans, sometimes you might need something in a hurry. Can your supplier accommodate this?

Ability to source new items.
Do they have a sufficient supply chain themselves that will enable them to source something out of the ordinary if you require it?

Ease of ordering.
Online, via telephone, fax (yes, some people do still use fax...!)?

Delivery days and flexibility.
Do they deliver once a week or can they deliver when you need?

Outlets that you can collect from if necessary.
Is there a branch locally, or within sensible driving distance, that you can collect from?

Terms of sale.
Invoice terms?
References required?
Credit arrangements?

Customer service charter.
What service do they offer to customers should things go wrong?

References from other customers.
No doubt they will require references from you; what references/testimonials can they offer to you?

Reputation.
What do others in your market place say about them? Are they known for their reliability and quality, or not?

Their future plans.
Expansion?
New product ranges?

You might be looking at some of these points and wondering how they are relevant to you. Let me explain.

You are about to start on an extraordinary journey of potential, where you will be exploring not only what you are capable of, but what your business is capable of too. If you want to achieve what you think you are able to achieve, then you will need suppliers on board who are of the same opinion. There's no point spending a long time building up a relationship with a supplier, only to find that they are unable to grow with your company and to supply what you need. Of course, there is a place for small niche suppliers, and they are often run by entrepreneurs just like you. Someone who knows their market inside out and grows with it. However, you also need to balance those small suppliers out with bigger companies who have the buying power you require. Some big companies get complacent as they become successful, and forget who their customer is, and what they really want. You only need think about the demise of Woolworths to realise that big does not always mean best.

Ensure that you have a number of suppliers, a mixture of large and small, so that you can always go to supplier two if supplier one can't supply what you need when you need it.

Premises

The business plan asks you to list any premises you are planning to rent, plus the cost of utilities etc.

When starting a business, particularly one that is based in retail or manufacturing, the first thing people generally say to me is, 'I will need to rent some premises.'

Not so.

I appreciate that for businesses that will require big machines, e.g. carpentry, you will need a workshop. That's a given. It can be difficult to operate such a business from a shed, although possible in the short term; provided you have scaled back the size of your machines (or have a huge shed!). However, even in these circumstances, you won't necessarily need a workshop all to yourself. There are lots of companies, particularly given the current economic difficulties, who are happy to sub-let a portion of their premises. There are also industrial estates in some parts of the UK that are given over to start-ups and micro businesses, so the rents are more affordable and there may even be mentoring and general support available as part of the package.

All these options are worth investigating further in order that you can keep any necessary costs down to an absolute minimum. There is nothing worse than getting into a long term contract (which most landlords will require) only to find a few months down the line that you could have rented a different workshop or other premises on a monthly basis at a much reduced cost.

For those who need a retail outlet, the first option is to see if you can operate from online first. Of course, if you want to run a coffee house or similar, that would be tricky, but for those who want to run a shop – this is a perfect start. Little investment, and much less in the way of weekly overheads.

Art and craft businesses often use sites such as Etsy to start their sales rolling. Other suggestions would be craft fairs, and local events. For making, again, local councils are getting into the arena of renting out space to craft makers and artists, so if you have large items of machinery that won't fit into a space at home, then it may well be worth speaking to your local council to see if they have such a scheme operating in your area.

Lots of mums run brilliant handmade craft or food businesses from home, hence the term 'Kitchen Table Businesses'. It conjures up evocative images of micro businesses being built and developed in the heart of the home – and is often not far from the truth. Some of our best known female entrepreneurs started working from home, including Jo Malone and Anita Roddick, alongside many lesser known local businesses that are headed up by women who wanted to garner an additional – or only – income for their families. Working with other freelancers and/or homeworkers, they develop into inspiring businesses by using their homes as their workspace.

If you just require an office space, then working from home is the perfect solution. Of course, for a single mum this is a great arrangement as you can keep an eye on your kids, and work at the same time. It doesn't take a lot of space, certainly not at first, and you could just set up your computer in a corner of your sitting room or dining room and get going. I wouldn't recommend using your bedroom; you really will need to get used to turning off your work at the end of the day, and working in the bedroom is known to disrupt sleep patterns – not what you need when you've worked hard all day long!

Some things to think about when working from home:

Have you notified your insurer?
Best to be on the safe side and check with your insurer that you don't need extra insurance to run your business at home. If clients aren't coming to your house then the chances are you will be fine, but you must make sure.

Have you notified the local council?

It is unlikely that you will have to pay business rates for the part of your house that is used for your business, particularly if it is being run in a communal part of the home, e.g. not a spare room where no one else goes, but you must check.

Have you notified your landlord?

Private landlords may allow you to work from home – very much dependent upon the landlord – but social housing providers are another story. You are likely to have signed a rental agreement that said you would not run a business from your home. Depending upon the business you would like to run, your landlord may be happy for you to carry on, but you must check and gain their permission in writing before starting.

Is it a requirement of your mortgage to notify your provider?

Check the paperwork and if so, contact them.

Make sure that you stick to a sensible set of working hours as much as possible, and are not tempted to work all hours of the day.

It's easy to get very caught up in your business and to work many hours more than the usual forty per week. Whilst this is understandable and probably necessary at first, remember that your business is also dependent upon your health. If you are working long hours with little opportunity to relax, chances are your health will suffer.

You must take time out to relax and do other things. You don't want to get to a point where your business is becoming successful but you are unable to keep up with the demands due to ill health.

Take time out to be with your family – don't let work consume your every waking moment.

It's important, whatever your home circumstances, that you spend time with your family, but never more so than when you are a single mum. If your children do not see their father, as my youngest son doesn't, then it is even more important that you share the time around.

Your children, whilst they will appreciate the work you are putting in for their futures, still need your interaction and input into their lives. Your business will still be there when your kids are tucked up in bed. Do what I've done, and many other single mums like me; work when your kids are in bed, or otherwise engaged.

Equipment

It is likely that you will already have some, if not all, of the equipment that you will need to set up your business – even if on a starter level before investing in more up to date and efficient items as you are able to. Most of us own a computer, printer and phone these days (vital pre-requisites for all businesses), and if you have already developed an interest, or been working in a particular business area, then you may well have some of the other tools you will need.

The business plan asks you to identify what else you might need and how much this will cost. Resist the temptation to go to the supplier catalogues and start to pick out the biggest and best of the items you require. At this stage, particularly given that you have no idea how the business will go over its first few months of trading, there is little point in investing huge sums of money in items you may never get full use of – and probably can't afford in any case.

Be canny.

The first port of call for anything that you need has to be liquidation sales. These are sales that result from company liquidation. Handled by auction houses on behalf of the Official Receiver and private insolvency practitioners in your local area, items belonging to companies that are no longer trading will be auctioned off. It may well be that you can purchase the resources you need at a fraction of the usual retail cost.

The next step, as previously touched on, would be to keep your eyes open for any businesses closing down in your area that may have items to sell. Often they will have a closing down sign in the window, and it just takes a bit of courage to go in and ask. You never know...

Thirdly, you could check the local press, as well as sites such as eBay. Buying privately is a great option and gives you the chance to check the item out and ensure it is working. Buying from online auction sites is not so user-friendly but you could ask to see the item first and check that it is up to the standard you require.

Buying second-hand is exactly what a canny start-up entrepreneur should be doing. Money is tight in the early stages, particularly if you don't want to borrow (and we will expand on this shortly), so the more you can save, the better. As long as you make sure the item works – and have it checked by an electrician or similar if you are nervous – you should be fine.

CASE STUDY

Neisa Reid

Neisa worked in accounts for over seven years, during which time she was made redundant – twice. Neisa decided to strike out on her own and now runs NTR Book-keeping Services. She is a single mum to two girls aged 12 and 15.

I set up the business in 2006 because I realised after my two redundancies that nothing is guaranteed in this day and age. I needed to provide for my family so I took my financial and employment status into my own hands. We do book-keeping, payroll, self-assessments, business planning, and some minor secretarial services. We've gone eight years so far, at a time when I have seen other businesses fail. I think we have stayed the course because of the good relationship I have built with my clients; I built a reputation for my business from scratch in an industry that is full of competitors. Most of my business is now on the back of their referrals. My biggest challenge has been trying to keep a work and family balance, as I often feel like I'm in a tug of war between work and family. I have managed to work around this through the relationship I have built with all my clients. Success will mean growing the business with like-minded staff who can give my clients the level of service I do, thus enabling me to spend more time with my girls.

Website: www.bookkeepinginbirmingham.co.uk

Chapter 10:
Your business – Finance

SECTION SEVEN: FINANCE

I have delivered a lot of sessions for people who want to start their own businesses over the last couple of years, and the thing that EVERYONE brings up at one point or another is money.

They usually have a couple of main concerns – how will I find the finance I need to set up, and how can I be sure that I have enough money to carry on trading each month through the difficult first year or two?

Of course, there are no guarantees when setting up a business (see the many points on unpredictability, risk and general not-knowing so far!), but there are some things you can do to lessen the impact of financial worries, as well as trying to money-proof your business so that you can at least be relatively reassured that the money stuff is under control.

For starters, too many budding entrepreneurs think that they need lots of money to start up their business. They don't. There's nothing wrong with starting small and building up from there, using free and almost-free resources to develop your business, and then using the profits when you start making them to replace and improve. Once you've set up one business and made the mistake of ploughing lots of money into it in the early stages, believe me, you won't make it again!

Now, I know there will be a lot of people reading this who are frightened of money. I don't mean a little nervous of getting the financial side wrong, or miscalculating a forecast here and there – I mean frightened – terrified, even – of money.

As someone who is both dyscalculic (as previously explained) and a single mum who has really been through the wringer, when it comes to money, I completely empathise. I know how it feels not to be able to understand basic sums; not to be able to compute what other people see as simple calculations, and to put off looking at financial projections – whether business or personal – just because they don't make any sense.

I also know how it feels to bury your head in the sand and hope that your memory is correct when it comes to bank balances and bills owing – and then to find that it isn't, and have to dig yourself out of the problem. And to then go to the other extreme and feel compelled to check your bank balance every day, sometimes more than once, just to be sure that you know what's going on.

For a single mum wanting to set up a business, the worry about money is even more acute. I firmly believe that a single mum takes the biggest risk of all entre-preneurs when starting a business because she has the most to risk – and the most to lose. This isn't a case of a single person wanting to run their own business – they only have themselves to look after. Or one half of a couple – there is someone else to help take the financial strain. It's someone who wants to better their prospects and those of their family, but is solely responsible for both their welfare and that of their children. Particularly if they receive no maintenance payments from their ex-partner, as a lot of us don't.

I think this is one of the reasons why many single mums don't feel able to set up a business, even though they might want to, especially when their children are young. The risk of what they might lose is too great, and the worry of scrabbling around for money without the safety net of benefit support or a full-time job can be simply overwhelming.

However, as I've said before, there is no reason to think that you have to give up a job to run a business (certainly not in the beginning, or whilst the business is starting to establish itself), and I know of lots of single mums who run their companies on a part-time basis very successfully. Similarly, if you are currently on benefits and keen to look into running your own company, there are schemes available to you. And, ultimately, don't forget that tax credits are also offered to those on a low income.

But back to the maths issue. Being able to deal with numbers when you run a business is, I'm afraid, necessary. At least to a basic degree. And the first thing you need to do, before you even start looking at spreadsheets and other financial information, is to deal with your numbers phobia – however it may manifest itself. Too many people set up a business thinking that, as long as they have a great idea that people want, it will be enough. That as long as they do the things they like to do really well, it will negate or cancel out all of the things they don't like to do. Or that if they find someone who will do the things they don't like to do (which is a brilliant, very positive move), then they won't have to worry about them at all. Not once. Not even a tiny bit.

Unfortunately that's not the case. Let me tell you why.

When you start up a business, you plan to a ridiculous level (assuming you do it properly of course!). You do a lot of scenario planning; if this happens, what will I do then? The more scenario planning you do, the more you get to know your business. How it will react to problems, what its strengths are, what its weaknesses may be – and you plug the gaps accordingly. What it can bring to the market that no one else can, and how that can be exploited. How it can develop from a tiny micro business with a couple of great ideas, to a business with staff and ideas aplenty.

You make it stronger by testing it. You give it the backbone it needs to survive pretty much anything.

When you really get into the planning, you become an expert on the market. There will be little anyone can tell you that you don't already know. You'll know the main players (and almost as much about their businesses as they do); the suppliers that those in the know go to, not just the big guys in the market; how the market itself fluctuates through the year and how you can counteract any problems that may cause; and everything that there possibly is to know about your customers.

And I do mean everything.

If you're clever, you'll take a leaf out of the supermarkets' book. You'll come up with loads of weird and wonderful ways of really getting under the skin of your customers (in a good way of course), so that you can almost second guess not only what they want now, but what they might be thinking they want in the future. And you'll get to a point eventually where you can dictate what they want! After all, when the first mobile phone came out (and I'm old enough not only to remember them but also to have had one), we just thought we needed to make calls with them. How little we knew. Apparently, given the levels of advancement in technology, we also wanted to take pictures, videos, go online, and get them to turn the lights on before we get home after a long day in the office – where they also give us our diaries, emails and allow us to keep in touch with colleagues across the world.

Now, at the time we didn't know that. But now we do. Who knows what else we don't know – apart from the phone manufacturers of course...

It's the same with the financial side of a business. You need to know everything that is happening in your business when it comes to money. What the balance of your account is each day; what is going out of it when, what is due to be paid when, and what your total sales are at any given time. Also what the total costs are of each of your products/services, and how much profit you will make. What the sales targets are each month and how close you are to them. Or, even better, by how much you have exceeded them.

Now, none of that requires an acute maths brain. It does require a level of organisation but it doesn't need you to be a whizz with numbers. A simple call to your bank will set up a weekly – possibly even daily – text to give you not only your business account balance but also the last six transactions. And a whiteboard in your office will enable you to list sales as they come in, so that you can see how on target you are.

Your accountant or bookkeeper will help you to calculate costs and profit for your products and services and, if you really don't think you can handle paying invoices along with everything else (particularly if there are a lot of them), then your accountant will also do that for you – but at a price remember.

Irrespective of how you feel about numbers, you must get your head around these small but vital things that you need to do. Being very honest with you, if you feel that you just can't do it, whatever advice or support might be out there for you – then don't! Please don't take the step towards setting up your own business if you can't fulfil these basic requirements. It's stressful enough running your own company without being scared of an aspect of it – and the financial side is so important that you really must feel confident about these tasks at the very least.

Have a read through this section, and see how you feel at the end.

Personal survival budget

You need to know how much money you need to bring in each month to cover your living costs and completing a personal survival budget is an essential part of start-up financial planning.

It will cover all aspects of your expenditure from rent/mortgage to utilities and even down to things like birthday cards and presents, and holidays. Remember, as with all planning documents, this is your survival budget so it needs to be personalised to fit your circumstances. Therefore, if there's a category missing – add it in. Don't bury your head in the sand and ignore an expense; the only person that you are kidding, in the long term, is you – and your financial plans will be wrong.

Once you've completed it, honestly, see where you can go back and cut costs. Do you really need to buy any clothes this year? Can you cut back on a subscription? This is the moment to pare back in the short term so that you can grab the chance to make more money in the long term.

Of course, as a single mum you probably don't have any spare capacity for cutting back but if you see one? Take it. The less you can take out as a salary or drawings, the easier on your business.

Of course, if you are setting your business up on a part-time basis whilst working elsewhere you may be able to bypass taking a salary from the business altogether, at least for a few months. However, still complete the plan; it will be a useful point of reference for the future.

Sourcing finance

Setting up a business requires money and/or resources at some level – that's a given. However, it doesn't necessarily entail borrowing to do it. I've set up five businesses, and every one of them was started without taking out a loan. I've worked with countless start-ups too and very few have resorted to loans.

It also doesn't always take a lot of money – another fallacy. Sometimes it can take just a few hundred pounds, or even less, to get started.

So what are the options available to you if you need money to start your business?

Savings

I appreciate that few of us have savings, particularly in a difficult economic climate. Savings are often either swallowed up to help get through until the situation eases, or they are ring fenced as untouchable. However, particularly if you are young, you may feel that if you have them – now is the time to use them.

Why do we have savings in the first place? What are we saving up for? Is it for a specific item – car, new furniture, university fees for children, house deposit – or perhaps just to have a sense of security in a rather uncertain world. Maybe the security of knowing that, whatever life may throw at you in a financial sense, you will have a better chance of coping with it? This is often the first pointer towards whether for you, using savings is the answer when setting up a business.

Risk has a big part to play in using savings. Remember I talked about the level of risk you might be happy with, and that some people are happier to take bigger risks than others. Never is this more obvious than when we are talking about using hard-earned savings to do something, potentially, very risky.

I would suggest that you sit down and look very carefully at your savings pot, and your current financial situation, and determine whether you can afford to use a small percentage of it. If you're not comfortable using savings, then don't. You aren't likely to look favourably on yourself, or your business, if you use the money and then wish you hadn't. And, of course, if you do use them then you will want to replace them at some point – and that might take some time.

I don't know about you, but having savings gives me a sense of security – no matter how big or small the amount – and particularly if you are a single mum. You want to know that if something goes wrong with the car, or the washing machine packs up, you can afford to repair or replace them. Not being able to do that, and being in a relatively perilous financial position for a while – where most start-ups will leave you – will impact not just on your feelings about your business, but may also have a knock-on effect on your confidence and self-esteem.

Please don't take the decision about using your savings lightly. Take time to think about it carefully, and talk to someone you trust to give you an unbiased view. It's not a decision you want to make and then regret later. Trust me!

Extra job

If you are in the position to be able to take on an extra job for a while, or perhaps to work extra hours in the job you already have, and use the money to start your business, then that may well be a great solution. Additional income, no matter how short term, is always useful as it can be the buffer you need both for the start of your business and for any resources that might be required.

Friends/family

Lots of people see friends and family as the answer to their start-up funding dilemma. It can be considered a perfect solution in some circumstances, certainly in terms of not having to approach a bank or other outside investor; plus you're able to stick with someone you know, trust and who may even have experience themselves of running a business, so can help with support and advice too. However, please be aware that it also carries a relatively high level of risk and disappointment.

Borrowing from friends and family will, by definition, often mean that you are digging into someone else's savings. They are showing their absolute faith and belief in you by using money put by for a rainy day or into a retirement pot to invest in something that, being realistic, could potentially fail and leave them out of pocket.

Now, only you know your individual friends and family circumstances and whether this is something that you are happy with – and I am certainly not going to tell you not to do it. But I do recommend that if you are planning to go down this route, you have a full and frank conversation with your potential investor about the risk involved. Explain that there may be a chance they won't get all of their money back; even any of it. If they are happy with that, then by all means go ahead.

You may want to draw up an agreement between you, detailing when you will make the first repayment instalment, how much it will be and what will happen if the person needs the money back in an emergency. This way, although it's informal and between two friends/family members, you are still being business-like about it. There is nothing worse than borrowing money on what you think is a relaxed, pay-when-you-can basis, hitting a crucial point in your business, and then having the bombshell of I-thought-you-were-paying-me-back-now to deal with. Knowing where you both stand is sensible and means that there's less chance of misunderstandings or falling outs – the last thing you want between friends and family members. Especially over something like money.

Business partner

Having a business partner is a good way to share the financial cost of setting up a business. In addition, with two of you working at the project, in theory this means you can get everything up and running more quickly. As the saying goes, 'two heads are better than one' – which can also aid decision-making and problem solving.

Of course, if there are two of you that means that the salary/dividend bill will be higher and there will be less profit to share around; however, most people in partnerships are happy to forego the extra income for the additional help, support and advice that their partner/s bring.

Don't forget that if you have a business partner, you will need to have an agreement between you in terms of roles and responsibilities, as detailed earlier in this book. Please ensure that you don't ignore this vital piece of start-up advice!

Venture capital/business angels

There are two types of outside business investor – venture capitalist and business angel. Watching TV shows such as Dragon's Den has made more of us aware of the work that venture capitalists do, and the success that they can bring to a growing company/entrepreneur.

Venture capitalists are usually interested in companies that have high-growth potential so, whilst they are less likely to invest in a brand new start-up than in a business that's been running for a short period of time and has a trading history, they are certainly worth approaching if you believe you have an idea with legs. They are usually organisations investing other people's money, rather than individuals investing in their own right.

Business angels tend to be wealthy individuals, often retired from their own companies with a track record in a particular industry, who wish to use their expertise and capital to help an early stage company to success. Along with investing money, they will work with the owner as mentor and advisor and, as they are well-versed in the trials and tribulations of starting and running a business, are perfectly placed to help.

Of course, an investment requires a payback and neither of these options are cheap. Both venture capitalists and business angels will require equity stakes, possibly substantial, within your company, and this is something you must weigh up against the obvious plusses of their overall involvement. Take advice from an accountant in terms of the stake you are prepared to release, plus ask a lawyer to look over any documents you are asked to sign.

Crowdfunding

Crowdfunding is a great way of getting finance for your business, and is particularly popular with those people starting a social enterprise. It's a way of raising finance by asking a large number of people, who will be registered on a crowdfunding site, for small amounts of money each. You upload the details of your company or project to the site, along with the amount of money you are looking for, and then potential investors approach with funding. The site itself will take a percentage of your funding as commission, although some may also charge a registration fee for the use of their site. If you don't reach your funding goal, you don't pay.

Investors like this as their risk is relatively low, only putting up a small amount of money for a project. It may also suit companies that may otherwise find sourcing funding to be problematic.

HP/Leasing

It often makes sense to consider hire purchase or leasing agreements for a substantial business purchase. However, in my opinion, it is never a good idea to take out a credit agreement for a start-up; particularly in the early months. Given that this is a risky venture, you want to keep your levels of risk in terms of credit to as close to a zero (if not always at zero) for as long as possible, whilst overcoming the usual ups and downs of the life of a new business.

Once you can see that the business is getting a foothold in the market and starting to stabilise, then reconsider by all means.

Grants

Free money is always a very welcome option for a start-up and grants are, essentially, just that. Depending upon where you live, your age, and other demographics, there could be a lot of opportunities out there waiting to be taken. Places to look include, of course, the internet, local council websites, national government schemes, charitable organisations (including The Prince's Trust if you are under 30), local enterprise partnerships (LEPs) and organisations such as UnLtd if you are setting up a social enterprise.

There will be many more grants available to those setting up a social enterprise/community interest company than those setting up a for-profit company. However, it is still worth doing some digging around to see what's available for your start-up.

Grants often have to be spent on specific things, or are for specific tasks, so be aware of this at the outset and don't apply for something that isn't applicable. Not only is fraud illegal but it doesn't do your reputation much good – and deprives a genuine applicant of funds to develop their own project.

Some grant givers will give you resources rather than the hard cash, and most will expect a report on how you have used the money. You must ensure that you cover off this requirement properly, and thoroughly; it is not in any way unheard of for organisations to request monies to be repaid if the receiving company does not demonstrate their proper use of it in accordance with the rules of the grant.

Overdrafts

Taking out an overdraft can be a great source of short term finance. However, it's very unlikely that you will be offered this as a start-up funding stream. Banks like to see some form of trading history before they agree to extend credit and are, despite their rhetoric, still very loathe to loan to new ventures – even more so if you've never run a business before.

Overdrafts are to be used to tide your business over those months when cashflow may be slow, and they can be a great stopgap. However, you should be able to prove that there will be money later in the cashflow forecast to repay this money – it's not a permanent solution. Apart from the fact that it's very expensive to use an overdraft (and that's assuming you've arranged it – an unarranged overdraft is subject to extraordinarily high penalties), the perilous nature of such arrangements does not lend itself to long term borrowing. Your bank can ask for repayment of an overdraft at any time and with little or no notice. Yes, that's correct. Little or no notice. The last thing you want to do is to borrow money in this way, only to find that you then have to repay it with just a week or two's grace – if you're lucky.

If you need to borrow money urgently, then you are best off ditching the idea of an overdraft, approaching the bank with a solid, well-written business plan and asking for a loan.

Loans

Life, in my experience, is full of 3am moments. Especially as a single mum. I know that I am preaching to the converted here – you will all be familiar with that time of the morning when you wake up in a panic, worries rushing around your mind, and find it difficult to get back to sleep. It's exactly the same when you run your own business – 3am becomes your best friend. The time is the same, it's just the worries that are different.

I'm not a fan of loans for start-ups. Not under any circumstances, if I'm honest, but I'm also a realist and understand that occasionally there may be no other choice;

particularly if you are setting up a business that requires machinery, for example. The key, therefore, is to ensure that not only do you borrow the very smallest amount possible in order to buy your resources/materials (not borrow to the hilt to buy everything brand new), but that you borrow at the lowest possible interest rate, with a payment holiday if possible – and that you understand the risks!

We've looked at the concept of liability and how this impacts upon you personally, particularly if you are a sole trader or in an unlimited liability partnership, so you need to be aware that if you take out a loan for your business under these circumstances, you personally will be liable for the money. The banks are very good at pointing this out in all fairness, but I want to do the same here too. Make no mistake, borrowing money is always a responsibility but as a sole trader? It's even more so.

In all honesty, the bank may be less keen to lend to you without the benefit of a limited company behind you. However, even with a limited company, they will still require a personal guarantee from you as director – so you are caught both ways! You are personally liable as a sole trader, and personally liable as a company director.

There are options for loans apart from the banks, of course. Some credit unions are starting to loan money to businesses – definitely worth checking out as their rates of interest are often favourable, and they are run for the benefit of the community so are more likely to loan to someone that the banks would turn down. They are my personal favourite for borrowing of any kind; their ethical operations appeal to me on many levels.

The other alternative is the well-publicised Start Up Loans scheme. Available through a number of delivery partners, the scheme has been very successful, claiming to have backed over 10,000 new businesses since its inception in 2012. As the scheme is designed for start-ups, and it is understood and accepted that the level of risk is higher, it is much more likely that your plan – assuming it is well written and thought out – will pass the rigorous assessment that all plans undergo.

Alongside the funding, businesses are also offered twelve months' free mentoring.

This is the part that often really appeals to start-ups and I have heard stories of potential business owners applying for small amounts of money, merely to access this invaluable help. I have also heard stories of loan recipients ignoring the mentoring side of the programme. This is not advisable! Those of us who have been running businesses for a few years would be delighted to be offered a free mentor. Not only are they experienced business owners/entrepreneurs themselves, but they also come with a wealth of hints and tips that they can pass on to you. Their support really is invaluable and I would urge anyone offered a mentor to grab the opportunity with both hands.

The only real downside to Start Up Loans is that the loan is packaged as a personal one, not a business one, so you are responsible for the repayments whatever happens to your company. However, the mentor is there to help you over those first few tricky months, so if you decide to apply for a loan and are successful, ensure that you take full advantage of their advice.

Selling stuff

Whenever I tell my sons that I am setting up another business, they rush to their rooms and slam the doors. I like to imagine that I can even hear furniture being pulled across the doorway. Why? My favourite way of raising start-up capital is selling everything that I no longer use, or am hoarding for the one day that I think it will be useful. Which is often never but I keep it just in case. You never know when you might move to a bigger house, or have a garden big enough, do you? As already mentioned, I've lost count of how many times I've sold my shoe collection – the pair I miss the most are the silver, bejewelled, strappy heels that I've never managed to replace – and my evening dresses left my wardrobe over two years ago now. (Well, if no one's going to take me out in them, I might as well sell them to someone luckier...!)

Raising capital using your personal property, the things that you probably don't need and can spare, is – in my opinion – the absolute best way of funding a start-up. What do you have to lose? A phone, a laptop you don't use, a few pairs of shoes, hardly-used CDs and DVDs etc. What great loss is that? Put them to good use and make something positive out of them. The risk is negligible. The sense of satisfaction immense.

Profit and loss account

A profit and loss account will give you a great, at-a-glance heads up on how your business will fair over the year – ending in either a profit or loss. Or a break even of course, which is the most that the majority of us can hope for in our first year.

Using your cashflow forecast as a guide, write in the income you expect for the year. Then calculate the variable costs to your business (those that rise or fall depending upon how many items you sell, i.e. raw materials) for that year. For instance, if your business bakes and sells cakes and you anticipate an income of £20000, and the materials to make those cakes will cost £5000 (flour, butter, sugar, cake cases etc), that is the figure you would use.

This then gives you your gross profit figure. You can calculate your gross profit margin from that if you wish.

Once that is calculated, you then deduct your fixed costs (those that don't change whether you bake one cake or one million), which leaves you with your net profit figure – what's finally left after everything is paid for. Obviously, in order to grow your business, you are looking for a positive figure here, but if you get a zero then that's all good. Especially for a first year.

Got a negative? Then you need to look at how you can redress the figures to get them to a zero or positive. Whilst there are some businesses that take a year or two to start making profit, as a single mum with bills to pay, you really want to be looking at a business model that can make some money for you as soon as possible. If you're unsure, take the figures to an accountant for advice. Remember, some accountants will charge, so either hire one who offers an all-in service, or go to one who will offer you a free one-hour appointment.

Budgets

In any business it's important to have budgetary controls in place, but never more so than when planning a start-up. The only way you can really keep a tab on what's being spent, and see where you might be overspending, is to carefully – and realistically – plan how much you will invest into certain areas and make sure that you stick to it!

There are two types of budget – income and expenditure. Both are self-explanatory but both have different functions and outcomes if you exceed the figures.

Exceeding an income budget is a celebratory event – it means that you have brought in more money than you may have originally budgeted for and this is a Good Thing! Income (or sales) budgets are always tough to forecast at the start of a business, but you should make sure that they are done and regularly reviewed. Remember what I said earlier in the book? A business plan is not a tick box exercise. It's a living document and, as such, should be regularly reviewed. Budgets are no different and, despite what you may do once your business has been running for a few years in terms of setting yearly figures, at the start you should be prepared to review on a regular basis, perhaps even weekly, in order to keep on top of the money.

If you find that you are not reaching your income budget each month or week, then you need to examine why. Is it your sales technique? Your marketing maybe? Or is your product or service not quite up to scratch? Perhaps you haven't identified the market properly, and need to do some more research to hit the right group on the head.

Or, are you just not putting in the time to develop your business? Believe me, you should be selling every minute of every day, particularly when you first start up, in order to gain the momentum you need to get your company from a standing start to a rolling run.

I searched through my emails recently to find a contact from when I first set up my business. I knew I had worked extraordinarily hard in those first few months, trying to make connections and develop leads, but had forgotten just how hard. In one day I had sent 121 emails. Yes, 121! All cold leads, all exploratory, all as a result of my 'spider brain' (start in one place with one idea, then see another angle and go down that road, which leads to another and another – you get the gist) – and not all of them came to anything but some did. And I am still working with them today. It was immensely gratifying to look back. It made me feel a little bit proud of my achievements.

That could be you! Scratch that. It will be you if you put the time in!

Perhaps you have just forecast your initial income budget figure too high? Is it, in reality, unachievable, and you've let your obvious and natural passion for your fledgling company take over a little? I've done that too. There's an easy solution. Go back and look at the figures, and this time take a dispassionate view. Take emotion out of it. Use your knowledge of the industry and ask yourself whether you would agree with these figures if someone else had shown them to you for their own start-up. Chances are, if you are struggling, you wouldn't.

If you set your income budget too high, particularly in those first few months, you will merely de-motivate yourself. You will work all hours for, seemingly, little in the way of results. Not a great strategy. Be realistic. Be honest. Be sensible.

The last thing you want to do is to overspend on anything when you first start up a business. The temptation is there, believe me – there are a million and one things you could spend money on – but you have to resist. Therefore, the perfect solution to that temptation is to set expenditure budgets for everything you think you will need to buy through the year. The cashflow forecast pro-forma will give you some ideas, but remember this is your business plan so you must adapt it where you see fit. Add in what needs adding in, and remove what's surplus to requirements.

Setting expenditure budgets is slightly easier than income budgets as you can research costs, often to the exact penny, so are able to give yourself an idea of how much you will need to spend as the business starts up and then grows. Make sure that you research a number of suppliers for an average cost of materials (take the middle of three as your best estimate), for instance; don't just go with the first quote. Be creative about where you can find machinery, tools and other capital purchases for sale without having to buy brand new. I often wondered, when making such purchases myself for my construction businesses, whether the value immediately depreciated by twenty per cent, just like a new car does when you drive it off the garage forecourt. Can you imagine if it did? What a waste of money! What else could you do with that cash? As I've said before, so much better to look for items via bankrupt stock auctions (contact local insolvency practitioners and the Official Receiver in your area for more details), online auctions (always make sure you check out the item before buying it) and using local knowledge. Companies will sadly fail as we know, regardless of the economic climate, so keep your ear to the ground and don't be afraid to walk into a shop premises, workshop or office that's announcing a closing down sale to see if there might be anything you can buy for your own business.

Another tip when it comes to budgeting? A golden one, given that you are likely to be overconfident on the company's abilities to make sales from day one – and that's not a criticism, merely a statement of fact:

When estimating sales, halve your final estimate.

When estimating expenses, double your final estimate.

Now, you probably think I've lost the plot but there's a reason I'm suggesting this. Forecasting for a start-up is extraordinarily difficult, and we've already established that you are likely to be full of positivity and a can-do mentality, so will believe that your business can achieve anything. In order to rein in that enthusiasm just a little, underestimating your sales and overestimating your expenses is a great ploy to start with. It ensures that you don't go spending lots of money you don't have; that you have a contingency fund for any unexpected costs (and believe me they will crop up) and, crucially, that you've planned for a worst case scenario. Just in case.

No amount of planning can take away the lurch in your stomach when you realise that your much-calculated and pored over cashflow forecast bears little or no resemblance to reality. I've been there, and I've had to pay the rent and feed my son on the back of it. At least having a margin of error gives you something to work with – and when you achieve way over your sales budget (because, let's face it, income targets are there to be beaten) and you dance around the sitting room in celebration (surely it's not only me who does that?!), you will be delighted that you took my advice.

Call me cautious, but anything to do with finance needs to be carefully thought through, and then thought through again. And anything you can do to protect yourself and your business, no matter how seemingly outlandish, is a good thing.

Cashflow forecast

I've made it pretty clear that I struggle with numbers and, being very honest with you, I find the next two parts of the financial section of the plan by far the toughest of the entire document. Give me a marketing problem and I'm in my element. An operational issue? Let me at it. A financial conundrum? Uh-oh... lie down needed...

However, light-hearted comments aside, this really is the most crucial part of the plan – without the money, we have nothing – so you must spend time and effort on getting it right. If you too struggle with maths then you have my utmost sympathy, but if I can do it, you most certainly can too.

The cashflow forecast is vital. Without it, you have no idea how your business will perform financially from month to month, and that's start-up suicide. There really is no point setting up a business if you aren't prepared to take the money side seriously; after all, it can impact on you on a personal level for years to come if you get it wrong.

By the time you've finished your first draft, and have written a few more, you should be able to read it like a book. At a glance, you should be able to identify potential issues for the financial wellbeing of your business and see where you will need to plug the gaps and shore things up – as well as where it all starts to look positive! It's a heart-warming thing to see, believe me.

So, we are looking at how the cash flows through your business – the income and expenditure – and where exactly it flows in and out. Based on that information, you can then not only plan potential future purchases, but also how you can develop and grow the business; where the positives are that you will want to build on, and where the negatives are that you will want to deal with.

The issue with the cashflow forecast is that it is just that – a forecast. You will likely have no real idea of how much income you will bring in and, whilst you can research expenses, it is still difficult to forecast them correctly. Again, this is where I remind you that a business plan is a living document and requires constantly updating – and never is this more pertinent than with a cashflow forecast. In my first year, I updated mine on a monthly basis and checked it every single week. Without fail. Even now, I regularly check my cashflow forecast to ensure that I'm on track.

Looking at the document itself, you will see that there is a pre start-up column, followed by monthly numbered columns. Most people write cashflow forecasts for a year to get an accurate picture of how their business is performing, and this fits with annual accounts and P&L accounts, hence the preference.

You will also see that there are two columns within each monthly column, headed forecast and actual. Please ensure that you complete both columns – this is not only extremely useful for moving forwards with your forecasting, but it also helps you to keep a check on how your business is really doing.

It's easy to forget that anything spent in the pursuit of starting a new business is an expense and, as such, should be included as an expense, which can then be written off against tax. Make sure that you save all your receipts relating to business activity, including rail, tube and bus tickets, cups of coffee for meetings, pens, paper, printer ink, photocopying costs – the cost even of this book! Anything at all whatsoever that is related to your starting the business can be given to your bookkeeper or accountant for them to work their magic.

You will see that there are some boxes at the bottom of the forecast that say, 'opening balance' and 'closing balance'. For a start-up, the opening balance would be zero. You have started a new business, so you have no money. However, any start-up capital that you put into the business would go into the box at the top marked 'capital/loans received'. It will then work its way through the document as any other income would.

When you get to the end of the pre start-up column, having also written in your expenses, you will be able to subtract the expenses from the income in order to achieve a final total. This total then goes into the closing balance box.

The closing balance of Pre Start-up Month becomes the opening balance of Month 1. And so the circle continues. Whatever amount of money is left at the end of one month becomes the amount you start with the next.

A few hints and tips for your cashflow forecast:

- Cash received from debtors is money owed to you. Let's say that you invoice in Month 1 but don't receive payment until Month 2. You then need to put that money into the Month 2 calculations.

- The forecast is looking at real-time information; when things actually happen, not when you think they might. So, if you thought you would invoice and get paid in Month 1 that sits in the forecast column. The actual would reflect the reality.

- Of course, if you are giving credit to all your customers then you will reflect this in your cashflow forecast. Remember that you will be paying for materials or other resources in one month but only receiving payment in the next. This can make for a difficult first year so think very carefully before you agree to such an arrangement.

It is worth remembering, as a general point, that the minute someone owes you money, you should chase them. They are now using your money to fund their own business – when you should be doing that yourself.

Have a very clear invoicing and collection policy. If you state money up front then that's when you collect. If you state payment must be received in seven days, then that's when you start to chase. Be reflective of the industry. If there are standard, expected terms then you may be better off working from those rather than setting your own.

Once your stated credit period is over, then you must have a policy in place to collect. I tend to email a statement across as a gentle reminder, which often works. On the rare occasion it doesn't, I then make a phone call. Only once have I had to resort to more serious tactics, and make use of the Late Payment of Commercial Debts legislation. It worked.

If you are in production, then it would not be an unusual thing to ask for a deposit up front, with the remainder being paid upon delivery. Or if a service, e.g. hairdressing, then a deposit upon booking and the remainder due upon the service being completed. You must ensure that you can at least cover your costs so that if the worst does come to the worst, you aren't too badly out of pocket if at all. Many small businesses fail due to customers not paying – try not to be in that position. Protect your business as best you can.

Remember too to allocate money for tax payments. There is nothing worse than having a good year, struggling the next and then getting a large tax bill on top of your problems. Allocate at least fifteen to twenty per cent of your monthly revenue and put it into a separate account. Take an accountant's advice on this.

Your cashflow forecast will show you where giving credit, or paying for supplies up front without collecting a deposit, may cause issues, and you can then decide how you might deal with it. In many instances it may be that you have to forego a salary that month. Can you do that? If you are running the business on a part-time basis, so your salary is being paid by your main job, then it may not be a problem. However, if you are relying on it as your main or only source of income then things are a little trickier. This is where you really must have everything tied down and planned out to the smallest detail to ensure that you aren't placed in that position.

Despite the school of thought that entrepreneurs and small business owners shouldn't expect to take a salary in the first few months of a start-up (which, from a development point of view, I understand), in the real world life isn't that simple and businesses have to pay their way. Whilst I am not advocating thinking that you can go from a nice salary in the corporate world to the same in your start-up (think again if that's your view – you really will have to cut back!), I do think that a business should be set up so that it can at least pay the person running it a basic salary.

Let's put it this way. Every one of my five businesses has managed it. With some careful planning and a lot of hard work and effort, yours can too.

Tax and VAT

As I've already mentioned, you must ensure that you, if you are a sole trader, or your company if you are a director, are registered for tax when you start trading.

If a sole trader, HMRC doesn't know that you are now running your own business so it's your duty to inform them. There is no excuse for not telling them. Everyone knows that they pay tax, so if you start trading, don't tell them and they find out (and they always do), then you are the one at fault. Be prepared for the consequences.

If a limited company director, HMRC will have been informed by Companies House, but if you haven't had a letter from them within two to three weeks of incorporation, it's always worth a quick call to your local office. Better safe than sorry.

The penalties for not complying with HMRC and the legislation are both expensive and fierce, and it's just not worth playing about with them. If you don't send in accounts, they can assess themselves – and you are then liable to pay. The onus will be on you to prove that their figures are incorrect; therefore, keeping proper books and records is imperative.

They do run training sessions so if you are unsure, get yourself along to one before you get too deep into running your company. Better to know up front what you need to do than to get it wrong and have to try to re-trace your steps.

Don't forget that you will also be liable to pay personal tax as well as company tax if you are a company director. I let my accountant handle all of this on my behalf. Company directors can take dividends as well as a salary, which is tax efficient. Your accountant will advise you on this once your company reaches year end and the final trading figures are available.

VAT is currently payable when a business's income during a cumulative period of the last twelve months goes over the threshold of £79000. If you think that you are heading towards that figure, then you need to register. You will charge VAT to all clients and customers and then re-claim any VAT that you pay when purchasing materials, resources etc. The difference is paid to HMRC.

Consult your accountant for more information and take their advice on when you should register.

General business requirements

Back office systems – you must ensure that you have invoices, letterheads and customer databases set up for your business. I have already mentioned the legal stuff that needs to be included on all documentation if you are running a limited company, so make sure that this is prominent.

You will also need to have some sort of filing system (envelopes and drawers don't count as a filing system), so invest in some folders and files and get that in place before you start trading.

Also make sure that you have a logical filing system on your computer so that you can access documents quickly. I now use a tablet as well as a pc, and sync everything across so that I can access anything I need wherever I am. It's proved absolutely invaluable on more occasions than I can remember.

Keep a running tab of expenses – enter them into your accounting software if that's what you're using, or an Excel spreadsheet – and make sure you do the same for mileage too. Check with HMRC for the relevant mileage allowance for your car.

Diary management – you cannot run a business without a diary. You might like to tell yourself that you can but you absolutely cannot. It's business suicide. Don't even think about it. Whether you use a paper one, or an online version, make sure that it is continually updated and that each and every appointment is entered correctly. I always make a point of putting addresses into my appointments, and a map if I haven't been there before, so that I don't get lost. Again, you can sync diaries across from a pc to a tablet or phone, so make sure that you look into this if it appeals. It makes life so much easier and saves having to have three different versions of the same thing – and it cuts down the risk of double-booking yourself (something I did a number of times before I found this handy app).

Bank accounts – you must ensure that you have a clear trail of money in and out of your business. If you are currently running a business as an aside, so not on a regular basis, then you may well be paying any money earned directly into your personal bank account.

Please stop.

You must either have a separate personal/savings account that isn't used for anything else, or a business bank account.

Most of the banks are much of a muchness; they all offer similar deals on business accounts (eighteen months' free banking initially), but some offer extras too – for instance, specialist start-up help, business bank managers in branch rather than at the end of a phone line (not all banks offer this!), free accounting software, dedicated bank managers for women starting their own business etc. It is worth visiting all the banks to make a decision on which is the one that appeals most to you, and offers you the best deal for your particular circumstances.

If you are looking at setting up a social enterprise – perhaps you want to run a community-based project – there are specialist accounts and even specialist banks who will support you. Check out Triodos Bank, for example.

Make sure that you keep all your bank statements safe and ready to hand over to your accountant at the end of the year, along with invoices and receipts. Whilst you can get free copies online, it will take time to organise – far better to keep the originals!

Companies House – I have talked extensively already about Companies House for those of you who wish to set up a limited company. Don't forget that there are inherent responsibilities that come with being a director and you must ensure that you fulfil them.

Add Companies House to your list of people to tell if you move; and make sure that all returns etc are sent back promptly. Of course, if you have an accountant they can do all of this on your behalf.

Employment laws – if you decide that you are going to employ someone, you will be subject to legislation in all steps of the process; from advertising the role, to interview, hiring and then employing.

I have already talked through the procedure around identifying the sort of person you are looking for, and how you should write a job and person spec, but you also need to ensure that you adhere to the law when you advertise and interview.

Businesslink is a great source of help in this area and you must research your responsibilities before starting the process.

For instance, you cannot discriminate in any way during the hiring and interviewing process – of course – but you might be surprised at what constitutes discrimination.

Health and safety: employees and customers – this is another area that is easy to forget but it's vital that you don't. You must ensure that, if you are employing staff or inviting customers onto your premises, you keep them safe.

Trading standards – all businesses are subject to trading standards regulations. Your products and services must do what they say on the tin. Trading standards are responsible for monitoring business activities around weights and measures, trade descriptions and product safety, amongst others. It is your duty as a responsible business owner to ensure that you trade within the law and do not dupe customers. There are severe penalties for those who do.

Executive Summary

Wow! You've finished your business plan. Or have you? There's still one thing to do.

Remember at the very beginning I talked about the Executive Summary – an overview of the whole business – and told you to complete that at the very end, once you'd written the plan? Well, now's the time.

So, the Executive Summary is exactly that. A summary of everything you have painstakingly researched and decided upon. Has anything changed as you've gone along? Do you still have exactly the same business idea that you started out with? The same suppliers, prices, costs, sources of funding? I'd wager not.

Now you need to re-read your plan, and write the Summary. This is a chance to really show your business off.

Talk about what it does; the fantastic person who will be running it (that would be you!), and why you are going to make such a success of it; the customer groups and how you will reach them; your suppliers and staff (if necessary), and give an outline of the financial aspects too; income, expenditure and profit where appropriate.

This will need writing and reviewing a few times before it finally reflects your business in all its glory, so don't be upset if the first draft isn't very sparkly and exciting. Ask someone to look through it for you and point out anything that doesn't read properly or flow very well. Be prepared to take a large amount of time refining before you have the final draft.

Once it's written and added in, sit down with a cup of tea and read – with justifiable pride – your fabulous business plan.

You have achieved SUCH a lot! Congratulations!

Be proud. Be positive. Be your dream.

Chapter 11: Presenting your business plan

Now that your business plan is written, you need to consider how you will present it to your prospective bank manager, as well as to potential business partners and investors.

The first thing you need to do is check for spelling mistakes, grammatical errors and financial miscalculations. All easily made but also easily solved. This is vital; remember what I said earlier about impressions. A mis-spelt plan, riddled with financial inaccuracies, will not impress anyone, let alone someone you want to bring into your business.

Once that's all checked and correct, you need to look at the presentation of the document itself.

Your front page should contain the logo of your company, a great first talking point, along with any other pertinent information, e.g. limited company number if you have one. You should have it bound professionally if possible, or find a suitable folder that shows the document off to its best. Don't think that rocking up to a meeting with your business plan in a plastic A4 file pocket or, even worse, with no cover at all and a paperclip holding dog-eared pages together, will cut it. Not only will any self-respecting investor show you the door, but you won't be demonstrating the professionalism you are supposed to as an entrepreneur/ small business owner; let alone the commitment and passion for your project that it deserves.

So, how do you present the information itself? This very much depends upon whom you are meeting, and who contacted whom.

If you're going to the bank, it's likely to be less formal than if you are meeting an investor – but formal nonetheless. They usually invite you to talk a little about your business before getting down to the account opening and other sundry things you may wish to discuss with them (insurances, for instance), so this is your chance to impress. A talk based on your Executive Summary is probably the way to go, and if you can demonstrate points using the plan itself then even better. It shows that you know what you are doing, and your plan, inside out.

If you are making products then why not take some along to show what you're doing? Take pictures if the products themselves are too cumbersome to put in your bag. It just adds to the overall presentation and is a really nice touch.

If you're meeting an investor, they are more likely to want some kind of formal presentation, either Powerpoint or Prezi. They will definitely want to see your products, so make sure that you have a range to show them.

Talk enthusiastically about your business; use your knowledge not only of the industry but of the market too – customers, competitors etc – to show that you are a worthwhile investment.

If you don't know the answer to a question, be honest. Don't pretend. Don't guess. Neither of those looks good. No one expects that you will know every tiny detail about everything (although you should certainly be the expert on your business), so don't worry if you are stumped for a response. Tell them you will come back with an answer within X amount of time – and make sure you do! It's very unprofessional, and not a good start, to promise something and then not deliver.

CASE STUDY

Tracey Longmuir

Thirty-nine year old Tracey is single mum to an infant son and lives in Lincolnshire, UK. After over 20 years in the print industry Tracey became an entrepreneur in 2011, running her own pet care business.

I wanted a change in lifestyle. I had employed a dog walker and pet sitter to help me look after my beloved dog when I worked long hours and worked away, and the idea of a dog walking business seemed something that would give me everything I wanted: the great outdoors, a more relaxed lifestyle and being around dogs all day every day. I had experience in marketing, advertising, managing profit and loss and I thought "I can do this, how hard can it be?" Isis Pet Care provides a one-stop shop for pet care from dog walking, doggy daycare, pet sitting, boarding, training and many more ancillary services and products. My branding and advertising has drawn a lot of positive comments and has stood me out from the crowd. I now employ eight people and I have secured investment to open a doggy daycare centre. My biggest challenges have been staffing, VAT, tax and securing grants and investment as well as managing my working hours, benefits and tax credits. Along the way I have learnt to trust my instincts, be more thorough in seeking out the right relationships (personal or business), that networking is key and to ask for help when you need it. Success to me is providing a good quality of life for my son. That includes having a fluid cashflow with no worries, a happy and motivated team, and satisfied and loyal customers. In the future I want to expand the grooming and training offering, and grow the new relationship I have with the local university, as well as expand the business.

Website: www.isispetcare.com

Chapter 12: Moving forwards

Success and failure

There is a fabulous quotation that I always use when working with start ups: 'Success is 99% failure', Soichiro Honda. We tend to get very hung up on failure in the UK, or certainly what we perceive to be failure. We are very hard on ourselves, and often extremely critical of those who have 'got it wrong'. You only need to read the papers or listen to the news to see the evidence. I find this attitude quite alarming.

Failure or 'getting it wrong' is good. It's the only way that we learn and grow; that we develop and move closer to what we really want. We find out what doesn't work for us, what doesn't make us happy – and what does – and we adjust what we do accordingly. Tell me how that can be a failure?

It's exactly the same with a business. As the owner, you make decisions and start along paths which then change, due sometimes to your business and sometimes to others. You may decide to close one area of your company so as to concentrate on another more profitable one. You may decide to look at other projects which stand more chance of success. You may find that, due to the actions of others, there is no point in carrying on your business. There are a million and one reasons why things go wrong and fail.

In my opinion, something can only be truly defined as a failure if you don't learn from it. If you do? Then it's a learning curve. A success.

Don't be afraid of things going wrong. Of things not quite running according to plan. That's what life is all about. You've dealt with much more in your life to date, of that I'm absolutely sure. This is just another chance to prove what you can do and achieve – irrespective of hiccups along the way.

Building you: keeping motivated

Running your own business is the most amazing thing you can do! Have I mentioned that before?! However, I would be the first to agree that it's tough, and there are times when you not only doubt the sanity of what you are doing but whether you can actually succeed. Whether you can overcome the challenges sufficiently to make a success of your business.

Add in to the mix that you are a single mum, juggling who knows how many other things, and you can feel as though you really are up against it at times.

However, it can be done. I'm the proof. My fabulous ladies who have agreed to be case studies throughout the book are the proof. And there are many, many more of us who have taken the challenge of starting our own businesses as single mums by the scruff of the neck, and made a success of them. Sure we've all made mistakes (I could write an entire book just on those), but we've seen it through and learnt from them. We've moved on and upwards because we believe in what we're doing. Because we love what we're doing.

How, then, can you stay motivated when you are stumbling? How can you see the light at the end of the tunnel when the battery in your torch has run out?

I guess it depends very much on you. What motivates you? What makes you feel that you can get back up and have another go? For some of us it's spending time with our friends and family, realising that there is more to life than worrying. For others, it's as easy as a hot bubble bath, glass of wine and a sneaky bar of chocolate. Only you know the answer.

For me, there are a number of things I do to keep motivated – not just on a business level but on a personal one too.

Firstly, I love music so, if I'm feeling a bit out of sorts, I will play it very loudly (sorry to my neighbours) and dance around the sitting room. I also love to sing, so I accompany any dancing with a bit of a sing-along, irrespective of whether I know the words or not. I've become very adept at using dah-dah-dah interspersed with the correct lyrics. Makes for a great performance.

If I'm really struggling, and I have those days too of course and sometimes more than one in a row, I'll dig deeper. My youngest son put a slide together for me when I first set up Operation Enterprise, showing me all the things I planned to do once I was financially independent again. There is a picture of a house in the town that I want to move back to; a very nice car (OK, I am a little susceptible to material things when it comes to fast cars). But more importantly, there are pictures of my kids, a smiling me, plus things I love to indulge in – music, walks in the countryside, fireworks etc. All the things I have promised myself I will spend more time on once I have succeeded with the businesses. Sometimes I will take a quick peek at the slide and it reminds me why I am doing what I'm doing.

I also re-read the testimonials I've received from people I've helped. There is no better testament to your success – whatever success means – than to see what others think of your product or service. Personally, I'm not interested in awards or accolades. I just want to know that someone somewhere has benefited from my help. That's it. Reading testimonials often leaves me emotional, teary even, but that's the point. It brings me to my senses and makes me realise that life could be so much worse – and has been so much worse – so I need to get back up and on with the job in hand.

Sounds harsh? I tend to be a proponent of tough love with myself; if I wasn't, I'd never have got through all that I have, to be honest, so I have no choice. But I don't necessarily advocate that for you. Be kind to yourself. Accept that we all have days when life seems unscalable and that perhaps this is your day.

Take some time out and watch the world go by. Often this can pay dividends, for it's the days when you take it easy that the ideas flow again – just what an business owner needs to move on to the next phase of their business.

Building your contacts: networking

Networking is a really important part of starting up and running a business, particularly when you are doing it on your own – and even more so when you're a single mum. Why is it more important for single mums than all mums, you might ask? Well, given the often isolated nature of being a single mum, it's a really great way not only to get out of the house to mix with those running their own businesses, but also to get out of the house to mix with anyone at all!

I have found over the years that I have been so absorbed by looking after my children, and then running my businesses, that I have neglected my own needs. I always forget that I need time to relax, to meet other people – new people. That putting everyone and everything else first is not emotionally healthy.

Networking for your business is a great way to get out there, to meet potential new clients, and even associates/freelancers that you could work with, or who could work for you as your company starts to grow.

There are lots of networks around, ranging from Chambers of Commerce, BNI and Mumpreneur groups, to more local networking groups such as First Friday or Curry Clubs (both of which are held locally to me) – details available online. This is where the search engines really come into their own! Don't be nervous of attending. I appreciate that it's a little scary to go to an event where everyone knows each other well, but they were all new once too. When you've been a couple of times, you will be chatting away to people as though you've known them forever; and the benefits of networking really can't be oversold. It's the one thing I recommend that everyone does.

Not only is networking a valuable business development tool, but it provides a great support network too. Everyone has times where their business struggles, and to be able to speak to someone else about it is a godsend. Don't isolate yourself. Get out there and make some friends!

You can also network online, of course. Popular options include LinkedIn, Twitter and Facebook. Twitter in particular has proved really useful for my businesses, gaining me not only new clients but also opportunities to collaborate. And new friends too! The value of networking online is often overlooked but I can highly recommend it.

Building your business — diversification

As your business starts to grow and develop, passing its first year birthday and moving on into its second year, you will notice not only how much it has changed from the initial business plan you wrote before you started trading (hate to say I told you so, but...), but also where there might be opportunities to start expanding and diversifying into other areas. All businesses have a number of areas of new revenue; sometimes it just takes a while to discover them.

Once they are apparent, you will need to write a new business plan. Of course, you will have been prepared to do this for the new financial year in any case, but you will need to explore these streams of income in more detail via a plan to see how you can exploit them to your best advantage.

If your business has been developing nicely, now might be the time to start considering the possibility of looking for new sources of finance. You now have a track record and a year's worth of accounts for a bank or investor to consider, which is a significant achievement. Remember how many businesses never even get to this point.

Customer service

Finding new customers is a very expensive business. Think not only of the marketing costs — often substantial — but also of the time involved that could be used for something else more profitable. Therefore, it makes sense to hang on to customers like grim death. Once you have them you definitely don't want to let them go.

Too many companies forget just how valuable customers are, and start putting their own needs ahead of those of the people who pay their salaries. In my opinion this is an elementary mistake, and a very short sighted view.

You need to look after them properly; don't treat them like numbers but as individuals — members of your family even. They should be your top priority. Whatever they want, they should get. No matter how difficult it may be to fulfil that need. I can absolutely guarantee you that this is the way to build a successful business.

Of course, there may well be a cost to that, which customers need to be advised of (and you need to ensure that you build it into your initial costings if top-notch customer service is going to be expensive in your particular business), but it doesn't cost anything to be friendly, to answer the phone within X number of rings, to respond to messages quickly and go the extra mile for their business. For instance, if they can only make an appointment to see you in the evening or at the weekend due to work commitments, that's what you should try to do. Make no mistake, if you don't someone else will – and in this day and age, grumbles and complaints about bad service can reach thousands of ears rather than a few due to the internet.

In my construction business, we developed such a fearsome reputation for both quality products and excellent customer care that we had a one hundred per cent repeat booking record – and an eighty-five per cent recommendation rate. Every single customer bought more than one product, and almost nine out of ten recommended us to a friend. We were even invited to parties at their houses so that we could sell our services to their friends! What other company can boast of such a record?

Word of mouth is the most effective marketing tool. It can't be beaten. If someone I know well recommends a company to me, I'm definitely more likely to rely on that recommendation than on a testimonial on their site – even though that too is a great demonstration of the company's reputation. If you treat your customers well, they will happily write you a testimonial. I haven't once had a customer refuse.

I also ask all my customers, and in my current businesses I ask students, for feedback on our programmes. Even those who have had a bad experience should be asked, for they are the ones who can really give you a heads up on what you need to do to improve. Don't ever be afraid to ask for negative feedback; it's where your most valuable learning comes from.

CASE STUDY

Niamh Kelly

Twenty-three year old Niamh lives in County Wicklow, Ireland. She is planning to return to college part-time in order to qualify as a make-up artist.

I remember when Mam started working for herself. She was really busy, she dressed better, and she was happier then she had been. We also had more money and went on our first foreign holiday. The downside of having an entrepreneurial mum is that she is regularly preoccupied. On the positive side though she is happy because she is doing what she likes doing. My mum has taught me that if you work hard you can achieve what you want to achieve. I would like to have my own business one day and she has inspired that in me. I'd like to have my own business as a professional make-up artist with a good client base. I also want to be responsible for my own financial future and not depend on a boss for it. However, I also think it's important to have a good balance between your personal life and your career. At some point in the future you need to be able to enjoy the success and if necessary take on a partner or hire a really good manager to allow to do this, and knowing when to do it is crucial.

Chapter 13: **The future**

'Be your dream' Ali Golds

So what will the future hold for you, as a single mum, running your own business?

I'd love to be able to say, happiness, health and all the stability you could shake a stick at. And, of course, I may well be right. For the sake of you and your family, I hope I'm right! However, there's a chance that I may also be wrong and things may not go quite according to plan. That's life, after all.

What I can tell you, for sure and with no hesitation, is this. If I look back at where I was in May 2005, it bears absolutely no resemblance to where I am today. In fact, if I look back at where I was six months ago, it bears little resemblance to where I am today.

My life has completely changed. And why? Because I took it by the scruff of the neck and instead of taking 'no', 'maybe', 'you can't', 'you shouldn't' and all the other limiting, disempowering and downright unhelpful phrases like them for an answer – I set the answers myself. In fact, I set the questions too. And then I set the rules.

Being a single mum is hard. Until you've been one, you have no idea just how hard it is. When you are part of a couple, it's Us Against The World. When you are on your own, it feels like it's The World Is Against Me. That's due in no small part to sections of the media and their overly negative attitude, but it's also down to the fact that your self-confidence has taken a hell of a battering. Who wouldn't find it difficult to be positive and go-getting, happy and smiley and all things sweet when, in many cases, their heart has been ripped out and unceremoniously jumped on from a great height – by someone who is supposed to have protected it?

And then they are left not only to pick up their own pieces, but to deal with their children's emotions too; without shedding a tear in public, and just carrying on as though life hasn't changed… 'Darling, Daddy has decided he needs to live closer to work but he'll still see you at the weekends…' And all the other trite excuses we trot out in the hope that we won't hurt our kids any more than they already have been.

Who would find that easy exactly?

Who would find it a walk in the park to get from work to the childminder or nursery at the end of the day in fifteen minutes, knowing that the journey takes twenty minutes in light traffic let alone rush hour, driving at breakneck speed so that they don't have to pay a late fine? Again.

(Assuming, of course, that you can work.)

Who would find that easy exactly?

Who would be able to walk into a benefits office to sign on without feeling utterly crushed and defeated having, in many cases, held down a successful job previously, or run a household with military precision whilst being celebrated for being a fantastic mum and partner? And now feeling more akin to a failure?

Who would find that easy exactly?

I could go on. If any of these scenarios currently resonate with you, or have in the past, or perhaps you're going through another that I haven't mentioned that is equally soul destroying, then you have my sincerest sympathy. I understand how you are feeling, from the bottom of my heart.

But do you know what? Being a single mum is also the most amazing thing you could be. I wouldn't swap my nine years of singlemumdom for the world. In fact, I'd go as far as to say that it's made me the woman I am today. I wouldn't have the fight, the courage or the conviction of thought I now have without having cried, despaired, struggled and crawled on my hands and knees through heartbreak to the degree that I have. Whenever I tell my story, people tear up. They find my tale of being in a women's refuge hard enough, without hearing about the betrayal by my ex-husband. They say that they can't imagine how I got through each day, and how I am still smiling today. They ask how I can possibly function on such an even keel, and with such passion.

I smile. What else would I have done? How else would I have survived if I hadn't carried on? How would my children have got through? Where would they be now if I hadn't determined to just get back up and start walking again? Someone had to take charge. Someone had to take control.

That someone was sure as hell going to be me.

As single mums, for everything that we do for our kids and for society on a wider scale, we deserve the best of everything. We don't get it offered to us but we certainly deserve it. But life is full of people who deserve the best of everything and don't get it, so we need to find it for ourselves. We need to get up and make something good happen.

And that's where running your own business comes in.

It gives you confidence. It gives you self-esteem and it gives you purpose. It gives you something to be proud of, and your kids something to look up to. I've lost count of the lessons my own children have learnt from my business experiences; how much wiser they are, and how much more prepared for real life than they would have been if I'd stayed in teaching. Running a business puts you at the forefront of challenges; right in the thick of chaos and turmoil on occasion too – but it gives you a fantastic sense of achievement, and a great living if you make it as successful as you possibly can.

I know that any single mum can set up her own business. I absolutely know it. I haven't yet met one who couldn't. It might not be today, or tomorrow but that doesn't mean it won't be one day. You've already got the skills – you just need the idea. And if you want to do it badly enough, you'll find the idea. Take something you love – a hobby, a passion – and put it to good use. Teach it in workshops; do it; help others to do it. Whatever it is, do it.

Let your future be your dreams. It can be done. I've proved it.

And as I continue on my way, still working towards buying my own home again for my children and my grandchildren, still working to change the lives of as many people as I can through my businesses, I will carry the lessons and the successes of my start-ups with me. The happiness when I take a booking for a new workshop. The moment of excitement when a business asks to meet me to explore partnerships and collaborations. The lump in my throat when someone tells me that if it wasn't for me, they wouldn't have been able to set up their own business and support their family. The delight when I look at my websites and marketing materials and realise that I did this. No one else. Just me.

I was the one who took nothing, and made something. And then used it to keep a roof over my family's head, and put food on the table. Gave my children a secure future, and myself my confidence. What better sense of satisfaction is there in life than that?

CASE STUDY

Yvonne runs YvonneB, a company that offers training services to large training organisations as well as direct training to women and small businesses. Early in 2004 Yvonne was made redundant from her job as Office Manager/PA to the Procurement Director of a chain of health clubs. Yvonne is 48 and she and her 26-year-old son live in London, UK.

I left that day in a state of joy and horror; joyful that the dry job had come to an end yet horrified by the prospect of finding another job. I was nearing 39, a single parent and I knew that 'just another job' wouldn't work for me. I settled into temping but was inspired by a magazine article on Virtual Assistants and decided to strike out on my own. Having been a PA it seemed like an easy transition to self-employment. My income fluctuated month to month and I struggled. My lifestyle didn't mirror the one I had created on paper but every time I considered going back to a job I felt sick… literally!

I watched my income plummet and my debts rise and all the while I tried to stay focused on building a sustainable business. I set up a network for virtual assistants and soon started to get calls from other women who had either been made redundant or who wanted to leave work and set up a home business. I was also part of a joint business venture providing workshops and coaching. But then came the recession… I went from living my dream to having no business and no income. I asked for help when I needed it (family and business associates who had more experience), taking temporary work when needed whilst I redeveloped my business. In 2009 YvonneB was created and launched in 2010, offering training services to large training organisations as well as direct to women and small businesses. I became an award-winning trainer in 2011 as voted by the UK's leading training company, Reed Learning. That was the first of many rewards I experienced for sticking with my decision through thick and thin.

Website: www.yvonnebltd.com

Acknowledgements

For my beautiful children who gave me my journey. Without you I'd be nothing. With you, I can conquer the world.

To my friend, and talented journalist, Alex Gray who wrote the fabulous case studies; and the wonderful Alexa Tewkesbury who took my raw manuscript and wove her editing magic all through it. Ladies, you have made me so proud. Thank you.

Thanks to my awesome case studies for sharing your stories. You are all inspirational.

And for all the single mums out there; those that I know and those that I don't. Believe that you can achieve whatever you desire, and it will happen.

About the Author, Ali Golds

Author Ali Golds is a small business coach and trainer, as well as Founder and Managing Director of Operation Enterprise www.operation-enterprise.com and The Juno Project www.thejunoproject.com. A seasoned entrepreneur, Ali has set up five businesses of her own since 2000 in a range of different sectors including construction, recruitment and now enterprise education consultancy.

Having worked as a consultant for a number of high profile organisations, including leading on a government review of enterprise education, Ali is often asked to speak, comment and write about a number of issues in the world of start-ups; with interest particularly focused on women and the challenges they face in becoming their own boss.

Three decades on from striding out into the world of work Ali has weathered many a storm, celebrated successes and overcome failure. In short, she has much to pass on to those following behind. Through her coaching programmes 'WorkIt' and 'Start up for Success' she supports anyone who wants to be their own boss; setting them on their personal road to entrepreneurial success.

www.aligolds.com

Made in the USA
Charleston, SC
16 June 2014